Other titles by Donald Honig
available in Bison Books editions

THE
October
Heroes
Great World Series Games Remembered by the Men Who Played Them

by Donald Honig

UNIVERSITY OF NEBRASKA PRESS
LINCOLN AND LONDON

⊛ The paper in this book meets the minimum requirements of American National Standard for Information Sciences—Permanence of Paper for Printed Library Materials, ANSI Z39.48-1984.

First Bison Books printing: 1996
Most recent printing indicated by the last digit below:
10   9   8   7   6   5   4   3   2   1

Library of Congress Cataloging-in-Publication Data
Honig, Donald.
The October heroes: great World Series games remembered by the men who played them / by Donald Honig.
p.   cm.
Originally published: New York: Simon and Schuster, c1979.
Includes index.
ISBN 0-8032-7286-3 (alk. paper)
1. Baseball players—United States—Biography.   2. World Series (Baseball)—History.
I. Title.
GV865.A1H6193   1996
796.357'092'2—dc20
[B]
96-2375   CIP

Portions of the chapter on Les Bell have appeared in a different form in *Sports Illustrated*.

Reprinted from the original 1979 edition by Simon and Schuster, New York.

For My Daughter Catherine

ACKNOWLEDGMENTS

THE AUTHOR would like to express his gratitude to the following:

The Card Memorabilia Associates, Ltd., Amawalk, New York, for assistance in photo research.

The National Baseball Museum and Library, and to the always helpful Jack Redding, in particular, for assistance in photo research.

In addition, the author would like to thank the Public Relations office of the New York Mets, with special thanks to Tim Hamilton, for the many courtesies extended. Also, the special contributions of the following must be noted: Joan and Theron Raines, Stanley Honig, Allan J. Grotheer, Edward Bartley, Michael P. Aronstein, Bill Henderson, and the steady editorial hand of Jon Segal. And, once more, thanks for the invaluable guidance and counsel of David Markson and Larry Ritter.

Above all, the author wishes to express his heartfelt thanks to the ballplayers who so generously and good-naturedly shared their memories with him, as well as allowed him to use pictures from their personal albums.

Pete Reiser scoring

Joe Jackson

Ted Williams

Al Simmons

Rube Marquard

Carlton Fisk

Tex Hughson

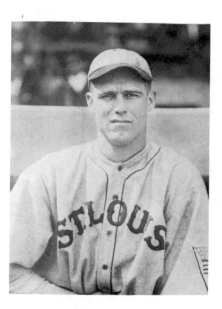

George Sisler

Rube Waddell

Chief Meyers, left, and Jim Thorpe

Riggs Stephenson and Babe Herman

Donn Clendenon

Home Run Baker

Mel Ott

Bob Meusel, left, and Irish Meusel

Virgil Barnes

Contents

(The dates in parentheses indicate the World Series in which each player participated.)

Introduction

THE WORLD SERIES remains America's premier sports spectacle. No sporting event so decisively enthralls the national consciousness as baseball's annual October pageant. Because of the length of the baseball schedule—162 games played over six months, beginning with the early buds of spring and ending in the grandeur of autumn—there is something heroic about the pitched combat of two teams that are at once survivors and winners, meeting to decide the world championship.

Given the mesmeric powers of the Series, nothing that occurs during that week in October goes unnoticed. Every pitch, every play, is made under the severest scrutiny, and baseball memory, which absorbs with relentless precision, catalogues the salient events with undiminishing vividness. Each Series is another stanza in an ongoing American epic. Reputations, and sometimes even careers, have undergone sudden and dramatic permutations. It happened to Gene Tenace—as he relates within these pages. After pursuing a steady if unspectacular career, Tenace suddenly erupted with astonishing devastation for one week in October and therein altered baseball's perception of him.

It is safe to say that no cynic has ever played in a World Series. Veteran pitcher Ed Lopat tells how he refused to leave a game despite an aching arm—and a 13–1 lead—because it was a World Series game, and that it nearly cost him his career. It was Lopat's homage to an event that is taut in its own perfect structure, that is rich in its own traditions, that is its own self-perpetuating myth.

The historical spectrum covered in this book ranges from 1908 to 1972. Smoky Joe Wood, who astounds us by saying that when he was a boy growing up in the 1890's there was no such thing as a World Series, remembers an inexplicable error of judgment on the part of the nearly flawless Christy Mathewson, which cost the New York Giants the 1912 Series. Ernie Shore recalls what it was like to pitch against young Grover Cleveland Alexander in 1915. Joe Sewell was standing a few yards away when Bill Wambsganss executed his blindingly sudden unassisted triple play in the 1920 Series, and Sewell was there again in 1932 when that great American original, Babe Ruth, called—or did not call—his famous home run in Chicago. Les Bell was guarding the line at third base when a now aging Alexander achieved his memorable strikeout of Tony Lazzeri in the 1926 Series. Bill Hallahan tells what it was like to pitch against the awesome Philadelphia Athletics in 1930 and 1931 and how a rookie named Pepper Martin became a national hero in the latter Series.

Fred Lindstrom, at eighteen the youngest man ever to play in a World Series, remembers a bad-hop ground ball that cost the Giants the championship in 1924. Phil Cavaretta still cherishes the few casual remarks made to him by Lou Gehrig in the 1938 Series. Lloyd Waner quietly but emphatically demolishes a long-standing legend about the 1927 Series.

Monte Irvin describes a stunned Giant team going into the 1951 Series against the Yankees a day after Bobby Thomson's home run. Tommy Byrne and Johnny Podres tell the story—as opposing pitchers —of the Brooklyn Dodgers' only World Series victory. Tom Seaver recollects the ultimate triumph of the Miracle Mets of 1969. Ted Kluszewski, in the twilight of a brilliant career, remembers the few days of heroics he achieved in 1959.

Since the format of this book bears the characteristics of an anthology, there naturally are omissions. The reader may note the absence of the reminiscences of Don Larsen, Cookie Lavagetto, Lou Brock, Bill Mazeroski, and many other October heroes. The ideal book of World Series reminiscence would be thousands of pages in length, for every man who ever suited up to challenge for the championship has tales to tell, be he garlanded star or anonymous fledgling.

Every Series in itself is a tale with beginning, middle, and end, and because there must be a winner, there must be a hero. Some of them are represented, or remembered, in these pages, which leaf back through the years and the decades of mellow remembrance, re-creating for one more encore the sounds and sights of baseball's treasures.

The October Heroes

Ernie Shore

ERNEST GRADY SHORE

Born: March 24, 1891, East Bend, North Carolina
Major League career: 1912, 1914–1917, 1919–1920, New York Giants, Boston Red Sox, New York Yankees
Lifetime record: 63 wins, 42 losses

Ernie Shore has come down through baseball history as the author of the most unusual perfect game ever pitched. This rare feat has tended to obscure what was a most successful, albeit brief, big league career. From 1914 through 1917, Shore was considered the ace of a Red Sox pitching staff that was notable for its abundance of talent. In 1915 he won 18 games and posted an impressive 1.64 earned run average. In World Series competition, Shore won three of his four starts, with a Series earned run average of 1.82.

I CAN'T tell you how many times it's happened in my life. I mention my name to somebody and they say, "Ernie Shore? You're the fellow who pitched that perfect game, aren't you?" That's the game that stands out in people's minds. But to tell you the truth, it was the easiest game I ever pitched.

It was on June 23, 1917, at Fenway Park, against Washington. Babe Ruth actually started the game for us, but he didn't stay in there very long. He walked the first batter, Ray Morgan. Babe didn't approve of some of Brick Owens' ball and strike decisions and let the umpire know about it. Babe got to jawing so much that Owens finally told him to start pitching again or be thrown out of the game. That seemed to set Babe off even more and he said something like, "If I go I'm going to take a sock at you on my way out." Well, Owens gave Babe the thumb right then and there. Ruth tried to go after Owens but a few of the boys stopped him, and a good thing too.

I was sitting on the bench and Jack Barry, our manager and second baseman, came running over to me and said, "Shore, go in there and stall around until I can get somebody warmed up."

You see, he never intended to have me go in there and finish the game. What he wanted me to do was go out on the mound and try to kill as much time as I could while he got somebody else ready in the bull pen. But there wasn't too much stalling I could do, because when a pitcher was thrown out of a ball game the next man was entitled to just five warm-up pitches. That's how it was back then; I don't know how they work it today.

I took my warm-ups and then started pitching to the next batter. Well, on my very first pitch, Morgan, the fellow Ruth had walked, tried to steal second and was thrown out. I threw two more pitches and retired the side.

When I came back to the bench Barry said to me, "Do you want to finish this game, Ernie?" My ball was breaking very sharply and he had seen that.

"Sure," I said.

"Okay," he said. "Go down to the bull pen and warm up."

So I did that and came back for the second inning. From then on I don't think I could have worked easier if I'd been sitting in a rocking chair. I don't believe I threw seventy-five pitches that whole game, if I threw that many. They just kept hitting it right at somebody. They didn't hit but one ball hard and that was in the ninth inning. John Henry, the catcher, lined one on the nose but right at Duffy Lewis in left field. That was the second out in the ninth. Then Clark Griffith, who was managing Washington, sent a fellow named Mike Menosky in to bat for the pitcher. Griffith was a hard loser, a very hard loser. He didn't want to see me complete that perfect game. So he had Menosky drag a bunt, just to try and break it up. Menosky could run, too. He was fast. He dragged a good bunt past me, but Jack Barry came in and made just a wonderful one-hand stab of the ball, scooped it up and got him at first. That was a good, sharp ending to the game, which I won by a score of 4–0.

Forrest (Hick) Cady and Ernie Shore in 1916

It wasn't until after the season that they decided to credit me with an official perfect game. There had been a little controversy about it because I had faced just twenty-six men. But they decided to put it in the books as a perfect game and it's been there ever since.

I didn't even know I had a no-hitter going, much less a perfect game, until I sat down on the bench in the eighth inning. Then one of the fellows said to me, "Do you know they don't have a hit off of you?"

Well, I didn't know.

"Maybe they'll get one in the ninth," I said. Then I laughed and said, "And maybe they won't."

They didn't.

A lot of my career was tied in with the Babe. In 1914 we were both pitching for Baltimore of the International League when the Red Sox bought us. Later on we both went to the Yankees. We were always good friends, Babe and myself. He was always a larger-than-life sort of fellow, even way back when. I guess there are more stories told about him than about anybody else in baseball. There's the one they tell about Babe using my toothbrush when we were roommates. Well, that's a good one, but it's not true. It was my shaving brush. I keep telling people the true story but they go right ahead and keep telling it the other way. So you can see how certain stories go on and on, whether they're true or not. When it comes to wanting to believe something, people can be very stubborn.

It's generally believed that Babe made his name in New York, with the Yankees. But they loved him in Boston too. He was always popular. One time we checked into the hotel in St. Louis. As soon as we had signed the register the clerk handed Babe a big basket full of mail.

"For you, Mr. Ruth," the clerk said.

Babe looked at it for a few seconds and then said, "The hell with it."

He went upstairs, leaving the basket there. I said to the clerk, "Let's open that mail and see what's in it."

Well, we opened it and among that pile of mail we found over a hundred checks made out to Babe, from people wanting him to endorse this or that product. I brought those checks upstairs to him but

Babe Ruth in 1915. "He was always a larger-than-life sort of fellow . . ."

he still wasn't interested. He told me to leave them on the table and he would look at them later. I don't know if he ever did look at them. Money didn't mean very much to him.

It broke Boston's heart when the Red Sox sold Babe to New York. But you know, I'd have to say that Babe belonged in New York. Given his abilities and his personality, that was just the place for him. He sure got the publicity there.

I liked New York myself, even though I was just a North Carolina farm boy. I was raised on my Daddy's farm. Originally he'd been in the liquor business. He'd been a distiller, until the state went dry sometime around 1906 or '07. Then he went into farming on a full-time basis. It was general farming—tobacco, wheat, peas, things like that. I grew up working on the farm. Did I like it? Well—no. You take work like setting tobacco with a peg, it just kills your back. It wasn't for me.

I went to Guilford College, which was nearby in Greensboro. Later on I did a little teaching there between seasons. Mathematics. My

Ed Reulbach

ambition was to become an engineer, but baseball killed that. In the beginning I had no idea at all of going into baseball, even though I always loved the game. I can still remember all the excitement at the college during the 1910 World Series. The Cubs played the Philadelphia Athletics. The Cubs had some great pitchers that year: Three Finger Brown, Orval Overall, Ed Reulbach. In those days you had to wait until the next day to get the score. You just stayed on edge until you finally got hold of that newspaper. I can remember one of the fellows taking out his pocket watch one afternoon and looking at it and saying, "Well, they're started. The game's on." That was about as close as you got to it in those days—knowing when the game was on and trying to imagine what was happening.

Baseball just sort of came upon me, so to speak. Pitching for Guilford College for two years I won twenty-four games and lost one. One day I was pitching against the University of North Carolina. It was the day after Easter Sunday, I remember, in 1912. The New York Giants were in town, working their way back home from spring training. One of the Giant ball players umpired the game and after it was over they made me an offer. It was my intention to finish college, but that offer to go up with the Giants sounded pretty good, so I took it.

I couldn't believe my eyes when I arrived in New York. Just an unbelievable place. Bowled me right over. All of those people, and those buildings, and those lights! You didn't know where to look first. Oh, I liked it. I liked it just fine.

Christy Mathewson

Christy Mathewson was still with the Giants then. I got to know him fairly well. He was a congenial fellow, and so was their other ace pitcher, Rube Marquard. No, I didn't talk pitching with them. I was just a rookie and they were way above me. In those days nobody taught you anything. You had to learn by observing. A rookie had to have a sharp eye and the capacity to learn on his own.

John McGraw? No, I'd better not tell you what I thought of him. We'll just leave that aside. Not my type of fellow. He was aloof, kept himself apart from the players. He could be very abusive too. Oh, no, he never bothered Mathewson. Mathewson was something special and McGraw never got after him.

I left the Giants because I wanted to finish college, which I did in 1914, before I joined the Baltimore club. No, I didn't want to play for the Giants. Not after what happened. You see, I was with the ball club all of 1912, pitching batting practice. Then when they won the pennant they sent me home before the World Series. They didn't want me to share in the Series money. That didn't sit too well with me, so I asked for my release and they gave it to me.

I had never followed any particular team. But I knew the names of most of the players, especially Walter Johnson. Everybody knew who Walter was. Later, when I was with the Red Sox I pitched against him. How fast was he? That's a hard question to answer, since most of the time you could hardly see the ball. But there was one game when I got two hits off of him. That was pure luck because I never got many hits. After the first one, when I came to bat again the catcher started to kid me. Then he yelled out to Walter, "Bear down now, this is a good hitter."

I laughed and stepped in. Darn if I didn't hit one like a bullet right past Walter. When I got to first he looked over at me and smiled.

"Say," he said, "you *are* a pretty good hitter, aren't you?"

But that was lucky. Walter was the fastest pitcher that's ever been up there. I never saw Smoky Joe Wood in his prime, but they told me he was just as good as Johnson. In 1912 Joe won thirty-four games and lost only five. But then shortly after that he hurt his arm. When I joined the Red Sox, Joe was still a good pitcher, though not as fast as he had been. But they said that in 1912 Joe Wood was as good a pitcher as ever lived.

Hitters? Cobb was a tough one. Lord, was he tough. But, you know, he wasn't the greatest hitter I ever faced. That was Joe Jackson. Why? He just hit everything you threw up there, that's why. And I mean he *hit* it. There's a difference between getting your bat on the ball and hitting it, if you know what I mean. He once lined a ball between my legs that didn't touch the ground until it got out behind second base. Good Lord, if that ball would have struck me it would have killed me.

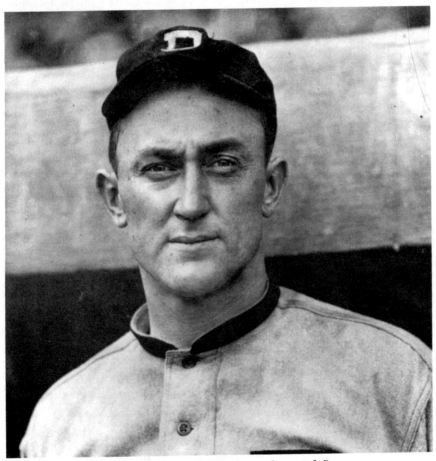

Ty Cobb in 1915. "Lord, was he tough."

Cobb, you see, was a scientific hitter. As great as he was, he still had to work at it. He would drag bunt, go to left field, punch it here and there. Jackson just walked up there and swung. And when he moved that bat it was the purest and most natural swing you ever saw. There was no way you could fool him with a pitch. Every time he put his bat on the ball it was a line drive. And they just whistled! If he had elevated the ball the way Ruth did, he would have hit just as many home runs as Babe, no question about it.

Best game I ever pitched? No, it wasn't any of the World Series wins. It wasn't the perfect game either. It was a game I pitched against the Tigers in Boston in 1915. On September 18, 1915, as a matter of fact. We were one or two games ahead of them in first place and knew we were going to have to stand them off if we wanted to win the pennant.

We went along to the top of the twelfth inning without a run being scored. I was pitching against Harry Coveleski. He was one of the best. Lord, I'll never forget that game. It was on a Saturday afternoon. We had the biggest crowd that had ever attended a ball game in Boston, up to that time. There were so many people we had to let them stand in the outfield, behind ropes. That was done a lot in those days. Mounted policemen patrolled back and forth to make sure the people stayed behind the ropes.

Ty Cobb led off the twelfth inning and hit a fly ball into the crowd for a ground rule double. So now I've got this holy terror standing out on second base with nobody out, with Bobby Veach and Sam Crawford coming up. That's a peck of trouble. And it was going to get even worse.

Veach put down a bunt and I fumbled it. That got Cobb over to third. Then I was looking at Sam Crawford. Well, I walked him on purpose to fill the bases.

They sent up Marty Kavanaugh to pinch-hit for George Burns. He hit one on the ground to Larry Gardner at third and we forced Cobb at the plate. Ty went in there like a lion out of a cage—that's the way he was on the bases—but we had him out with plenty to spare.

The next fellow was Ralph Young. Well, I gave it everything I had and he grounded into a double play. When I walked off that mound I got a mighty nice cheer from the Boston fans.

Then in the bottom of the inning we scored a run and won the game. That was the best I ever pitched, and not only because I shut them out for twelve innings, but because we were fighting them for first place and needed that game. It helped take some of the steam out of Detroit and get us into the World Series.

I was certainly looking forward to pitching in the World Series. We had a great team on the Red Sox in 1915. One of the best pitching staffs ever: Rube Foster, Babe Ruth, Joe Wood, Dutch Leonard, myself. Carl Mays was on that staff too, but we had so many starters he had to stay in the bullpen all year. You look at the records of that staff sometime. The highest earned run average any of us had was around 2.4. And we had one of the best outfields anybody ever saw—Tris Speaker, Harry Hooper, Duffy Lewis. And fellows like Dick Hoblitzell, Heinie Wagner, Everett Scott, Larry Gardner, Jack Barry. Just a fine team. Bill Carrigan was the manager and he was tops. Best manager in the world. He was close to his players, and he had their respect. I never heard a man ever speak ill of him.

Carrigan told me I was going to open the Series, which was just swell with me, and quite an honor considering the talent we had on our pitching staff. No, I wasn't a bit nervous. Why should I have been? There were only three things that could happen—I could win, I could lose, or I could tie. That's what I always told myself when I went into the pitcher's box. So there was nothing to worry about. And when I had my good stuff I nearly always won. I was a fastball pitcher. I threw a ball that dropped, a natural sinker. And it dropped fast, too; real fast. When I had it going for me they hit nearly everything to the infield, very seldom to the outfield.

I drew a pretty good opponent for myself in that game—Grover Cleveland Alexander. One of the best. He was one of the first pitchers to throw what they call a slider today. He threw a live fastball too, and had good control. The Philadelphia papers were filled with praise for him. He was their ace and they were very proud of him and were counting on him. They called him Alexander the Great, and he surely was a great one.

Alex beat me out in that first game. I can tell you just how it happened, too. It's sixty-three years ago as we sit here today, but I can remember it as clear as anything. I told you they didn't often hit me to the outfield. Well, in the eighth inning I gave up a couple of runs and not one ball left the infield the whole inning.

The score was 1–1 when we went into that last half of the eighth. With one out I walked Milt Stock. Then Dave Bancroft came up. He hit one right on the nose to Jack Barry, who made a terrific stop of it. But Everett Scott didn't cover second base, to this day I don't know why. Maybe he didn't think Barry would get it. When Barry wheeled to throw to the base, nobody was there, and he held the ball just long enough for Bancroft to beat it out.

The next man walked and the bases were loaded. Then Gavvy Cravath stepped in. He was the great home run hitter of the day, you know. He had hit something like twenty-four home runs that year, which was the new record for a single season. If I tell you that Cravath hit more home runs that year than most *teams* did, you'll get some idea of what a slugger he was. So you can bet I was careful with him. I got him to hit one on the ground, but the best we could do was get him at first, and a run scored.

Then a fellow named Fred Luderus came to bat. He hit a little nubber toward the mound. Well, it had rained the night before and the grass was still wet and slippery. In fact they had burned hundreds and hundreds of gallons of gasoline on the field before the game to try and dry it. It helped some, but not enough. I went after the ball and my feet just flew out from under me and down I fell. I still had a chance to throw him out but the darndest thing happened. You see, in those days they had a path from home plate to the pitcher's box, a skin track without any grass on it. You don't see that anymore. With the ground so wet from the rain, there were spike marks in that path about an inch deep. Well, the ball hit one of those marks and curved right on away from me. All I could do was sit there and watch that little white ball roll away—so slowly I could see each stitch—while

Grover Cleveland Alexander in 1915. "They called him Alexander the Great..."

the run crossed the plate. Talk about bad luck. I should have been out of that inning without a run scored. You put their hits end to end and they still wouldn't reach the outfield grass.

Alexander said after the game that I pitched in hard luck, that the breaks went against me. Well, he was right about that. The other run they scored came in the fourth inning, on a slow roller hit by Possum

Whitted that he just did beat out. And wouldn't you know it was the only hit Whitted got in the Series? But you shouldn't complain about those things. You get your share of the breaks too, and then it's the other fellow's turn to moan. Anyway, Alexander pitched a beautiful game against us. Just because you were *unlucky* doesn't necessarily mean the other fellow was lucky. Alex worked a fine game and he deserved to win.

In the top of the ninth we had a man on first and one out and guess who came up to pinch-hit for me? First time he was ever in a World Series. Babe Ruth. Babe told me later that he was trying to hit one out to tie it up for me, but the best he could do that time was ground out.

President Wilson was there the next day. He was the first President ever to come to a World Series game. As a matter of fact, we had to delay the game for about twenty minutes until he showed up. There was some grumbling on the bench about that, because the boys were all warmed up and set to go and then had to sit down and wait. But it worked out all right because we won that game, and we won the next one.

I came back to pitch the fourth game, against George Chalmers. I beat him, 2–1. That was the third straight game we won by that score. I'll tell you how we scored one of our runs, just to show you how those breaks even out. In the third inning we had a man on first and Chalmers fell while fielding a bunt. Later on in the inning Harry Hooper beat out a slow roller to score a run. Just stay in there long enough and keep believing, and you'll get your share of the breaks.

In the sixth inning, Duffy Lewis doubled home the second run and I held on to beat them. Lewis was the best hitter in the pinch I ever saw. In the game that we beat Alexander, we got the winning run in the last of the ninth. With a man on first they walked Speaker on purpose to get at Lewis. That was a sad mistake. I never will forget it. As he walked up to the plate Duffy turned around and said to us, "Watch me hit that first curve ball." Well, that's just what he did. He waited for the curve and hit it right by Alexander's ear, over second base and into center field.

A very unusual thing happened in that World Series. When we

moved back to Boston we didn't play our games in Fenway Park; instead we played in Braves Field because the seating capacity was so much greater. We drew over forty thousand for those games in Braves Field, which was a new World Series attendance record up to that time. Nobody complained about the shift because it meant more money all around. The winner's share amounted to $3780 apiece. That was a year's pay for a lot of people in those days.

We won the fifth game in Philadelphia and that gave us the championship. Just to show you what a strange game baseball can be, we won that game on home run power—Duffy Lewis hit a home run and Harry Hooper hit two. What's so strange about that? Why, over the course of the whole season we hit only fourteen home runs. That's right, fourteen home runs for the whole season. Then we go into that last game and hit three. Hooper hit as many that day as he did all year.

I was looking forward to getting back home. It's a long season you know. I went back to Yadkin County in North Carolina and spent the winter hunting quail. Was I the big hero in town? Well, there was no town. I lived five miles from East Bend, out in the country.

I took the train out of Boston the day after the Series ended. Went to Greensboro, and from there caught another train to Winston-Salem. From Winston-Salem I went to Donaha. That was the railroad station. Nothing there but the depot. I was the only one who got off the train. My Daddy was waiting for me with the horse and buggy. He took me home.

I was glad to be home. You look forward to the season opening, you look forward to winning the pennant and getting into the World Series, and then you look forward to getting home again. I think that's pretty good—to always be looking forward to something nice.

We won the pennant again the next year, in 1916. There was a Red Sox dynasty in those years. Boston won the pennant and the World Series in 1912, 1915, 1916, 1918.

In 1916 we played Brooklyn. They were called the Robins at that time, after their manager Wilbert Robinson. It was the first pennant ever for Brooklyn and, yes, I'll say there was some excitement about it. They had brass bands parading and the flags were flying and I guess

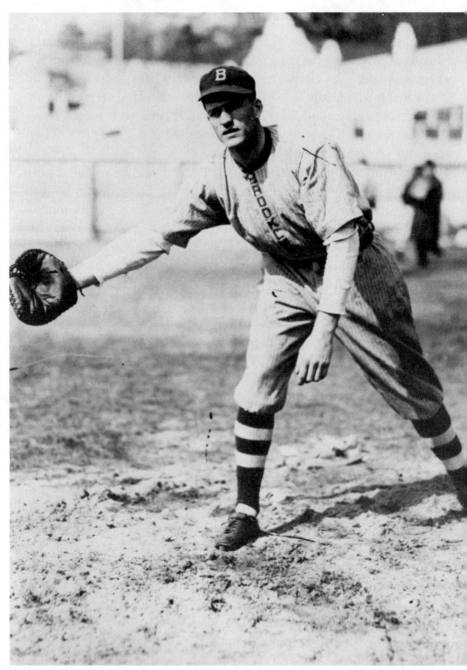

Jake Daubert

just about everybody in Brooklyn was worked up over that World Series.

Brooklyn had some of the old Giants I'd known during that year I spent with New York, fellows like Chief Meyers, Fred Merkle, Rube Marquard. Rube opened up the Series for them. He was an awfully good pitcher, Rube was, but we peppered him in that game. I was pitching for the Red Sox and had them beat 6–1 going to the top of the ninth. I had very good stuff that day. Too good. The reason I say that is because my ball was breaking so much I had difficulty in controlling it. In the ninth I walked a few men and hit one and they scored four runs. Fell just one shy. We won it 6–5.

The second game is probably still the best ever pitched in a World Series. You know who the pitcher was? Babe Ruth. That's right. By that time Babe had developed into a great pitcher, just great. He won twenty-three games for us that year. And what a game he pitched in that Series! In the first inning he gave up an inside-the-park home run to Hy Myers. And that was all he gave them. We got the run back in the bottom of the third—Babe knocked it in himself with a ground ball—and that's the way it stayed.

Sherry Smith pitched quite a game himself, for Brooklyn. It went to extra innings. Babe shut them out for thirteen innings, until we got a run in the bottom of the fourteenth to win it. He was quite a boy, the Babe, wasn't he?

Brooklyn had a few rough hitters in their lineup. I'm thinking of Zack Wheat and Jake Daubert, although I don't recall that they hurt us too much in that Series. The fellow who gave us the most trouble was Stengel. That's right, Casey was playing right field for Brooklyn. Casey always had something to say, even in those days. I remember, just before the first game, during batting practice, Duffy Lewis and I were walking across the outfield and as we passed him Stengel said, "Hello, boys. What do you think your losing share is going to come to?"

We just laughed at him. We didn't think it was possible for anybody to beat us. Our pitching was too good. Why, we had five strong starters. Along with Babe and myself, there was Rube Foster, Dutch Leonard and Carl Mays. The five of us started just about every game that season.

Brooklyn won just one game in the Series. Jack Coombs beat Mays in the third game. Then Leonard won and I came back to beat them again in the last one, against Jeff Pfeffer. He was a twenty-five-game winner for them that year. The score was 4–1. I had my good stuff that day and pitched a three-hitter. The only run they got came in on a passed ball. I still remember that pitch. It broke so much it missed the catcher's mitt entirely. That's what my fastball would do. It sank awfully sharp and sometimes the catcher couldn't handle it.

My ball was breaking so sharply all through the Series that Wilbert Robinson couldn't believe it. He said later that I was putting licorice on the ball and then sticking dirt to it. Not true. I never did that in my life. And I told them so. But Robinson didn't believe it. He said those low pitches were taking too many funny shoots. They kept asking to see the ball the whole time. I was glad for them to do it; it gave them something extra to think about. But I wasn't monkeying with the ball. I didn't have to. What they were seeing was the natural break I had on it.

The nice thing about that last game was we won it right at home. Our fans let go a really good shout for us when it was over. We got a standing ovation. It was the third world championship the team had given them in five years and they showed that they appreciated it.

The Red Sox should have won a lot more pennants in those years, but they didn't. That's when the Yankee dynasty started, in 1921. I can tell you about that.

You see what happened, Harry Frazee, who owned the Red Sox, kept getting into debt because of theatrical investments that weren't panning out. He was always in the need of cash and he found the right man in Colonel Ruppert, who owned the Yankees. Ruppert had plenty of money and he desperately wanted a winner. Up to that time the Yankees had never won the pennant. New York belonged to McGraw and the Giants, and Ruppert wanted to change that.

So with those show business losses keeping Frazee in the soup, he started selling players to the Yankees. I was one of the first to go, along with Duffy Lewis, in 1919. My arm was shot by that time and I didn't play but one more year and not a very good year at that. But then Frazee started selling them one after another. Over the next few years do you know who he sold to New York? Well, Ruth of course. And then there was Everett Scott, Wally Schang, Joe Dugan, and all of those pitchers who won pennants for the Yankees—Carl Mays, Herb Pennock, Sam Jones, Bullet Joe Bush, Waite Hoyt. Every one of them were twenty-game winners for the Yankees at one time or another.

So when they talk about that Yankee dynasty, I always say it was really a Red Sox dynasty, in a Yankee uniform.

Tommy Byrne in 1947

Tommy Byrne

THOMAS JOSEPH BYRNE

Born: December 31, 1919, Baltimore, Maryland
Major League career: 1943, 1946–1957, New York Yankees, St. Louis Browns, Chicago White Sox, Washington Senators
Lifetime record: 85 wins, 69 losses

In spite of frequent lapses of control, fastballer Tommy Byrne was one of Casey Stengel's most dependable pitchers when the Yankees launched their awesome onslaught upon the American League in the late 1940's and 1950's. After two 15-game seasons, Byrne was traded around the league and actually returned to the minors before resurfacing with the Yankees in the midfifties. In 1955 he had his finest year in the big leagues, winning 16 and losing 5 and leading the league in winning percentage.

Up to that time Brooklyn had never won a World Series, though they sure had tried a hell of a lot of times. I was aware of the fact, but I couldn't have cared less. I was pitching that seventh game for the Yankees and I had other things to think about.

That's the game you always dream about when you're a kid. I think any kid who ever wanted to be a ball player has pictured himself in the seventh game of the World Series, winning it with a strikeout or a home run.

You try to be professional and not notice the pressure; but it's there, it's inescapable. I remember this one incident, it happened just prior to the game. Somebody from *Sport* magazine came into the clubhouse and said to me, "Tommy, if you win this ball game there's a good possibility you might be Most Valuable Player of the Series. We've got a Corvette sitting outside and we've got to give it to somebody."

Duke Snider

"Thanks for reminding me," I said.

Then he probably went over to the Dodger clubhouse and told Johnny Podres the same thing. Johnny was starting for them and both he and I had pitched complete game victories earlier in the Series and the feeling was that whoever repeated would probably get that car. Just one more thing to think about, right?

I had won the second game of the Series against the Dodgers in Yankee Stadium. Stengel had told me he'd written me in for that game. I'd had a pretty good year for him in 1955—16–5—and knew he would find a spot for me somewhere in the Series. Let me tell you about that Dodger ball club—they were no picnic and particularly not for a left-hander. They were all good right-handed hitters with the exception of Jim Gilliam, who was a switcher, and Duke Snider. They were murder against lefties, but Stengel figured that those wide-open spaces in the Stadium would, to a certain extent, neutralize some of that power. He didn't want to start his left-handers against them in Ebbets Field, which was tailor-made for that Dodger club. So he started Whitey Ford in the first game in Yankee Stadium and Whitey beat them. The next day I got the ball.

The Dodgers scored first, in the top of the fourth. But in the bottom of the inning we rubbed that out and then some. Gil McDougald opened with a hit but was erased on a double play. That's when we got down to serious business, with two out and nobody on. We started sniping at Billy Loes. I remember there were hits by Yogi Berra and Elston Howard and Billy Martin and a couple of walks in there and we had two runs and the bases loaded. It was my turn at bat and I was in a fine spot to help myself. Loes went to two balls, no strikes and I sort of had to be looking for the hard one. Sure enough, that's what I saw and I hit it into center for two more runs. That sewed up that baby. We won it 4–2.

It had taken me a while, but I had finally won a World Series game. I'd been in baseball for nearly fifteen years at that point and it was a nice feeling to put one of the big ones in my bag. And just to put a little icing on it, I was the only left-hander in about a year to start and finish a game against Brooklyn and win the game. That tells you something about how fierce they were against lefties.

Then the Series moved to Ebbets Field. Johnny Podres beat us. That fellow hadn't completed a game since June, but he sure as hell completed that one. Pitched a nice, steady ball game and stopped us, 8–3.

Then they beat us the next two in Ebbets Field and all of a sudden we're down three games to two. But now we're going back to Yankee Stadium. Still very confident, of course. Look, after you've been good

Mickey Cochrane, left, and Schoolboy Rowe

enough to win a pennant over a long season, nothing that happens in a few games, World Series or not, is going to destroy that confidence. I remember somebody asking Stengel about his pitching plans after the fifth game.

"Ford in the sixth game, Byrne in the seventh," he said. That's the way Casey was thinking. That's the way we were all thinking.

And that's the way it happened. Whitey Ford beat them 5–1 in the sixth game. We got all our runs in the first inning, before the first hot dog had been eaten. We figured after the fifth game that it would have to go seven because down three games to two we could no longer win it in six. That was the Yankee attitude in those days. Pride and confidence. An ongoing thing with the Yankees, decade after decade. It was the thing that made me sign with them in the first place.

Actually Detroit was my favorite team when I was growing up, and at one time I nearly signed with them. When I was seventeen, they brought me up to Washington from my home in Baltimore to work out with the ball club. Then they asked me if I wanted to finish their eastern swing with them and then accompany them back to Detroit.

Babe Herman, left, and Hank Greenberg in 1937

Charlie Keller, Joe DiMaggio, and Tommy Henrich

You'd better believe I said yes. All of a sudden there I was, traveling with and pitching batting practice to guys like Hank Greenberg, Charley Gehringer, Mickey Cochrane, Goose Goslin, Jojo White, Gerald Walker, Pete Fox, Rudy York. I was with them that August in 1937 when York hit seventeen home runs to set a record for a month's production. They had some real fine pitchers too, like Tommy Bridges, Eldon Auker, Schoolboy Rowe. Everybody was very nice to me. The Tigers wanted to sign me, but at about that time I was offered a full scholarship to Wake Forest and decided to take it. That eventually led to my signing with the Yankees, so it worked out all right.

I guess that decision to go with the Yankees was sort of preordained. They were the great team when I was growing up. A lot of youngsters were attracted by the Yankee legend in the 1930's and wanted to play for that ball club. It was Ruth, Gehrig, DiMaggio, all those pennants and World Series. It was New York, Yankee Stadium. This was where the money was, where the crowds were, and I figured if I could play big league ball the Yankees were the team I ought to play it with.

Part of the Yankee success lay in perpetuating the image. From the moment you signed a contract with them they began instilling in you that Yankee tradition, and they never stopped, not even when you were with the parent team. The attitude in those days was so great it was unreal. If we had a ball player on the Yankees who seemed to be doing things on his own, who didn't appear to have had bred in him what it meant to play and win as a team, he wasn't around too long. There just was too much talent in the farm system. In those days the top Yankee farm clubs at Newark and Kansas City were stocked with players of major league caliber. They just wouldn't allow anyone, no matter how much ability he might have had, to tarnish that Yankee image. It meant too much, in ways that were as much practical as symbolic.

One of the main men behind that constant striving for pride and perfection was Mr. Weiss. George Weiss. He was head of the farm system and then became general manager. One of the finest minds ever to come into baseball. He could be tough, but I liked him very much. He never lied to me. There were times when I might have been unhappy with him and he less than happy with me, but we were always very frank with one another. The wrangles were over money. Sure. What else? But I would have to say that generally he was fair with me. I certainly have not suffered by my association with the Yankees. I was always proud to work for them, and for Mr. Weiss.

Mr. Weiss knew that success would breed success—a fairly obvious proposition, but it wasn't all that easy to keep it going year after year in a highly competitive business like baseball. He was also a stickler about that "Yankee image," and he worked hard to maintain it, another job that wasn't too easy, particularly in a business where the personnel are constantly changing.

Listen, you've got to remember we're talking about a dynasty that wasn't a five-year thing, or even a ten-year thing. This went on for more than *forty* years. From 1921 to 1964, to be exact. How many pennants did the Yankees win over that span—twenty-nine? Twenty-nine pennants in forty-four years. Now, it's got to take more than hot bats and strong arms to do that, to keep it going. So you have to believe it when I tell you there were some intangibles mixed in with it.

I think you've almost got to have been part of it before you can really understand what that Yankee pride was. You know, when Stengel first came to the ball club in 1949 I don't think that even he —with all his years of experience in the game—grasped the reality of that pride. But he saw things happen in that first season that made him proud to be a part of that organization. I think the spirit and the determination and the pride really astounded and impressed him. He found out that there were a lot of people working not *for* him but *with* him to win that pennant.

Let's look at it this way. Every game we played, before we went out on the field, we knew the other club was using the best pitcher they had available. We never saw a patsy. Everybody wanted to beat the Yankees. That juiced us up and gave us added incentive. So when the season finished up and whether we had won by one game or ten games, we knew we had earned it. Looking forward to every challenge thrown at you, that's what keeps feeding that pride. And unless you had been around and played on other clubs, you couldn't really feel the full extent of it.

I'll tell you another thing about that ball club. If you were a young player sitting on the bench, a utility man, you would generally find one of the older players who might not be playing that day sitting next to you during a game and talking. They would start pointing out certain things that were occurring on the field, telling you what to anticipate and how to be ready and what to do. Men on first and third and one out, for instance. The ball is hit to you in the infield. Do you go home with it or do you try for the double play? They would tell you how to think about that: what's the score, the inning; who's pitching; how hard is the ball hit, how fast is the batter? And so on.

When I was walking all those men and the fans were beginning to wonder when Old Byrne was going to run out of bases on balls, there were people trying to help me. And not just the manager and coaches and other pitchers—but fellows like Charlie Keller and Bill Dickey. They spent an awful lot of time with me, talking to me and catching me, trying to help. That's what the Yankees were all about. One helping the other. Passing along the tradition. If you had the ability and wanted to learn and to be part of a unit, brother, you were in the right place.

When I first joined the Yankees I could throw as hard as anybody, but I was wild as a bull. Along with the live fastball, I had a good curve, but it was a matter of getting them over, otherwise what good were they to me? The funny thing was, I never really believed in my own mind that I was so very wild. I didn't think I was "losing" wild, if you know what I mean. I used to feel that if they let me pitch I wasn't going to give more than three or four runs a game, and I would get a couple back with my own bat, because I could hit.

But it was true, too, that I put them through so many agonies—ball one, ball two, ball three. Walk a guy. Strike out a guy. Walk two more. Strike out two more. That's the way it went. I led the league in bases on balls three years running. But I didn't give up many hits, and I had years like 15–7, 15–9. Then in '51 they traded me to the Browns. The story was that Dan Topping, one of the owners of the

Casey Stengel in 1922. "The guy was just a ball of fire."

club, grew so exasperated watching me pitch that he finally lost patience and traded me. I don't think either Mr. Weiss or Stengel had anything to do with it. In fact, Stengel was pretty unhappy about it. We had a nice talk shortly after the trade.

"Casey," I told him, "the greatest thing in the world for me would have been to start a Yankee and finish a Yankee. But how many people really get to do that?"

He commiserated with me and I told him not to worry, that I'd make a buck. I wasn't bitter and he appreciated that. He was an unusual person, a great guy. I thought he was a good manager and liked him just fine. Some of the boys didn't cotton to all the platooning. In Casey's first year, 1949, we won the pennant on the last day of the season, and I remember some of the boys saying that we won it in spite of him. But I think they forgot about all the injuries we suffered that year and I thought Casey juggled and manipulated his players very skillfully.

I really think Casey was at his best when things were tough, when it was close, either in the ball game or in the pennant race. The guy was just a ball of fire. If we had a five- or six-run lead he could sit on the bench and practically be snoozing—you hardly knew he was there. But let us be a run or two behind in the sixth or seventh inning, and he'd come up off that bench and start yelling and hollering and throwing left hooks into the air and the first thing you know he's got the whole team following suit and everybody is putting out a little more.

I thought I understood him a little better than a lot of the other guys did. We were both left-handed, you know. I read somewhere once that only one out of every twenty-eight people are left-handed. It's a right-handed world. We're discriminated against. I'd like to have a buck for every time I was called a "crazy left-hander" by somebody. How many times have you ever heard anybody called a "crazy right-hander"? That's discrimination. You ever see a left-handed water fountain? There you are. So you have to do so many things differently that eventually you become a little different. Sure I believe that.

A lot of left-handers are extroverts. Casey certainly was. So was I. I was known for my antics out on the mound. Sometimes after walking a few batters I'd look over toward the bench at Casey and smile. People might have thought I wasn't being serious out there, but I was serious as hell. Casey knew that. He was pretty calm most of the time. But Jim Turner, our pitching coach, would get nervous. He was a serious sort, Old Jim was.

I'd get these streaks of wildness and all of a sudden I hear footsteps behind me. It's one of the infielders. Maybe Collins or Rizzuto.

"What do you want?" I'd ask him.

"To talk," he'd say.

"What do you want to talk about?"

"Nothing," he'd say. "They motioned me from the bench to come in and talk to you. They're probably warming somebody up."

"Well, I don't know why," I'd say. "I've only walked two men and not missing by more than a yard."

Then I would look over at the bench and Turner would duck his head and Casey would fold his arms and look up at the dugout ceiling. They knew we were talking about them.

Then I'd turn to the infielder and say, "So you've got nothing to say but just came over to kill the clock a little."

By that time the umpire is heading out to break it up. The infielder retreats and I go back to work. Maybe it looked like I was horsing around out there, but believe me, I wasn't. It was my way of staying loose and maybe keeping my infielders loose. If I would have started moaning about my control it might have tensed up the guys behind me.

Some times I'd talk to the guys in the opposing dugout. You'd be surprised how your voice carries out there. I would do that to disrupt them, get them mad. You get somebody mad and it becomes that much harder for them to concentrate. You break a batter's concentration up at the plate and you've stolen a little edge. I might say something personal to them, though never to the point where it was offensive. I might ask him how his family was getting along or something like that. Most guys can't stand that sort of thing when they're getting ready to hit. Occasionally I'd keep talking to them even as I started my windup. Some guys were really unnerved by that.

Now and then as a guy was stepping into the box I'd ask him what he was hitting. If he said he didn't know I would go into my windup and say to him, "According to this morning's paper you're hitting .280," or whatever his average was. Some guys got so agitated they jumped right back out of the box.

There were some hitters I had trouble getting out. So when they came up I would tell them, "Fastball. Right down the middle." And I'm telling them the truth. I figured, hell, if a guy doesn't know what's coming and he's hitting me, I might as well tell him. And do you know, sometimes they stopped racking me up. Al Rosen, over there at Cleveland, he just wore me out, year after year. Finally I told myself I was going to work on him. Tell him the truth. That's what I did. He started popping them up to the infield. Boy, you should have seen him! He'd run down to first base calling me everything under the sun.

You try to get that edge, and at the same time try not to let them get it on you. I remember one time I was brought in to pitch to Ted Williams. As I was taking my warm-ups I noticed Ted moving closer and closer to the plate. He wanted to see what my ball was doing, you see. Well, I didn't like that, so I winged one at him to run him away from there. He didn't appreciate it one bit. I could see him growling. I had pretty fair success with Ted over the years; I don't think he made his living off of me. But he was all hitter, and you'd better believe that.

But there was one guy who did steal an edge on me—as well as on a lot of other pitchers—and I didn't know about it until a couple of years later. Remember Bob Dillinger? He played with the Browns. A singles hitter who could run like hell. Well, I could never get him out. He was always pinging base hits off of me. But do you know what he had done? He had planed down one side of the meat end of his bat about an inch and a half to make it flat. Hell, you do that and you're hitting the ball square and not getting so many pop-ups. But nobody noticed it because he had painted it over and lacquered it up. One day he hit a ball and there was a play at home and Yogi picked up the bat to throw it out of the way and he felt the flatness. He showed it to the umpire and that was the end of Dillinger's flat bat. But for a while he was whistling line drives all over the place with that thing.

No, I didn't get a sense of being sent into exile when they traded me to the Browns. It's true there was no greater tumble in baseball at that time than going from the New York Yankees to the St. Louis Browns. But I didn't think it was so bad. You're getting a fresh start, right? No place to go but up, as managers of last-place teams always like to say. Frankly, I enjoyed playing there for that year or so. I was playing for Bill Veeck, you see, a man I always felt was great for baseball. I had a mediocre year, something like 7 and 14, but the next year when I got my contract there was a raise in it. Beautiful.

I was traded from the Browns to the White Sox. One day, not long after the trade, we came to New York to play, On a Sunday afternoon we're playing the Yankees, the game is tied, the bases are loaded, and I'm sent up to pinch-hit for Vern Stephens. I caught hold of one and hit it out. Grand slammer. The White Sox were in first place at the time—this was in June. We get on the train that night and at one of stops, I think it was Philadelphia, the public relations man came over to me and told me I'd just been traded to Washington. They were in last place at the time, so there I went again, taking a header from first to last.

Then Washington let me go to the minor leagues. Do you know why Clark Griffith released me? I was 0–5, true, but he said he wasn't disappointed in my pitching—it was my hitting. He had gotten me because he wanted me to do some pinch-hitting along with my pitching and my bat had turned cold. How many pitchers do you know who've been let go because they stopped hitting?

I generally was able to swing the bat pretty well. In fact, when I came out of the service in '46, the Yankees wanted me to go to Newark and play first base. They didn't have anybody at that time they were really set on for first base and wanted me to give it a crack. I had hit .328 over at Newark one year, pitching and playing a little outfield and doing some pinch-hitting. But I'd had a very good year on the mound before going into the service, winning seventeen and losing only four. If I hadn't had that success I might have thought about switching to first base, but having had the good year I didn't want to give up. I felt I was too close to being a big league pitcher.

Actually, playing first base would have been easier. Pitching is much harder work, and if you've had a bad outing you have to wait four or five days to redeem yourself. Pitching for the Yankees could be tough, too. You were expected to win. Lose a few games and you were apt to find yourself in the bull pen. I used to kid the outfielders, telling them they ought to pay to get into the ball park. They could have two or three bad days and nobody would notice. But if a pitcher has two or three bad days that finger starts to point at him. But I loved to hit. One year I hit .326 with the Yankees and I started kidding the out-fielders, telling them I was doing their work for them. They told me if I was getting paid to hit it might be a different story. Well, maybe.

You want me to tell you something I've thought about for a long time? Listen to this now. When you throw the ball hard and it gets there quick and has a lot of action on it and is around the corners, the hitter's not too sure if it's a ball or a strike. There are a lot of pitches that are so close it's unreal. Believe me. Now, the first guy who should be able to tell whether it's a ball or a strike is the catcher. The second guy who should be able to tell is the umpire. The third guy who should be able to tell is the pitcher. The fourth one is the hitter.

You see catchers complaining more often on ball and strike calls than hitters. But they don't like to make a fuss with the umpire. They'll crouch down there and grumble into their masks. That happens more times in a game than the fans realize. The reason they do it quietly is they don't like to show up the umpires and they don't like to change the tempo of the game if the pitcher is doing well.

The hitter steps into the ball, the ball has got some movement on it and he's a trifle uncertain and lets it go right on by him. If the hitter is uncertain, maybe the umpire is too. Is he always so absolutely positive when the pitch is very close? But what happens more times than not when the umpire can't make up his mind? He calls the pitch a ball. Why? Because he's got to raise his hand to call a strike, but do nothing if it's a ball. In other words, by doing nothing he's done something. That split second delay becomes a commitment and he's called a ball.

My contention is they ought to have to raise their hand on a ball too. It's just too easy to call a ball. On a close pitch all the umpire has to be is indecisive for just a second and it's too late, you've lost the pitch. How often do you see an umpire look a pitch over carefully and then call it a strike? I can tell you why you don't often see it—because they like to be crisp and decisive out there.

This is not to be critical of umpires. Most of them are very good and bear down all the time. It's just my feeling that if they were made to raise their left hands and call those pitches the pitcher would get a fairer share of the close ones.

In 1954 I was pitching for Seattle in the Pacific Coast League and had a good year. Won twenty games. In September the Yankees bought me back. I joined the club in Baltimore, won a game and then we headed for New York. When I walked into Yankee Stadium the next morning, do you know who was standing outside to greet me, other than the doorman? Dan Topping, the fellow who had got rid of me three years before. He had a big smile on his face.

"Glad to have you back," he said, giving me his hand.

I thought that was beautiful. He didn't have to do that.

A year later I had my best season in the majors, 16–5. Not only that, but I'm handed the ball in the seventh game of the World Series.

As I said, I was aware that Brooklyn had never won a World Series; but I don't think I gave that fact more than a passing thought. I was more interested in the Yankees winning than I was in the Dodgers losing, if you know what I mean.

The game started off quietly. We made a run at them in the last of the third but saw a good opportunity go by the boards because of a bad break. With two out we get men on first and second and Mc-Dougald is the hitter. Now, with two out the Dodger third baseman, Don Hoak, is playing deep and protecting the line. McDougald hits one not very hard toward the bag. Hoak is playing too deep to get the ball and throw him out. No way can he make the play. But here's Rizzuto sliding into third and as he does the ball hits him. It's a single for McDougald but Rizzuto is automatically out. So instead of the bases loaded and Berra coming up, the inning is over.

The Dodgers got a run in the top of the fourth and then another in the top of the sixth. That run in the sixth was the key, because of the maneuvering that Walter Alston did. Reese opened with a base hit. Then Snider laid down a bunt. I fielded it and threw to Skowron at first. We had Snider out but Skowron dropped the ball. That was the play, right there, for more reasons than one.

Roy Campanella came up and he sacrificed the runners to second and third. Then I gave Carl Furillo an intentional pass to load the bases. At that point I left the game and Bob Grim came in.

Gil Hodges flied out, Reese scoring after the catch. Then Don Hoak walked, loading the bases. And here's the key maneuver. Alston sent George Shuba up to hit for Don Zimmer, who was playing second. Best move Alston ever made in his life, and not because Shuba got a hit. Shuba in fact made out. But when the Dodgers took the field in the bottom of the sixth, Gilliam had to come in from left field to play second and Sandy Amoros went to left field. Sandy Amoros. Boy, they'll never forget him, will they?

So now it's our half of the sixth. First two men get on. Billy Martin and Gil McDougald. Yogi is next. Just the man you want up there in that spot, right? One thing about Yogi: He almost never hits the ball to left field, and certainly not down the line. One of the most pronounced pull hitters in the game. But didn't somebody once say baseball is a funny game? Yogi hits it down that left field line, and I mean right down the line. From where I'm sitting in the dugout it looks like it's got to hit the grass in the corner and probably bounce in for a ground-rule double.

The runners take off. Nobody anticipates that Amoros can catch this ball. But, unbelievably, he does catch it. And in my opinion the reason he did was because he was out of position. He should have been playing Yogi farther over toward left-center. He had no business being where he was. There was a gap in left-center you could have marched an army through.

So Amoros runs and runs and at the last split second sticks his glove out and catches the ball a step or two away from the barrier. And there's Pee Wee Reese, perfectly positioned to take the relay, waving his arms and yelling for the ball. He's about to nail McDougald. Gil had gone around second base and he had too much ground to recover.

Pee Wee Reese in 1940

Yogi Berra

He had to stop in his tracks and turn around and start running again, and with those Dodgers throwing line drives to each other there just wasn't time. He had gone much farther than he should have. Martin, who was on second, didn't go that far off the base. He didn't have to, because if the ball falls in he can still score. Of course Martin and Frank Crosetti—who was coaching third—had a different angle on the ball. From McDougald's angle it looked like it was going to fall safely. That's the way we saw it from the dugout, from an angle approximately the same as Gil's.

Amoros makes the good peg to Reese, Reese whirls around and whips the ball to Hodges at first, doubling off McDougald. That broke our backs.

Now if the other guy, Gilliam, had been out there, I don't think he could have caught that ball. Gilliam was right-handed, you see; he would have had to reach across his body to get the ball and I just don't think he could have done it. Amoros, with the glove on his right hand, just did barely make the catch.

That was the crusher, right there. We took a little run at them in the eighth, but Podres got out of it. Johnny pitched a great game. And I mean, he *pitched*. I'll tell you how he beat us. Very often, on 2–0 and 3–1 counts, when you had to be laying back for the "cripple" —the fast one over the plate—he was throwing changes. And getting them over. We were popping them up or hitting them nowhere. If you can get that change-up over in a cripple situation you're going to get a lot of guys out. Hitting is all timing, you see, and if you can throw a guy's timing off he's going to hit the ball where you want it to go. And if somebody decides to get cute up there and start looking for that change, he's just as apt to see a fast one ripped by and be caught flat-footed.

Johnny didn't strike out too many, but there sure as hell were a lot of pops and grounders. And let's give Campy some credit, too. He was the fellow calling the game. He called for those straight changes in key spots at least a half-dozen times and Podres had the courage to throw them. They did a hell of a job and let's give them credit.

Some people said the Dodgers were lucky because of that Amoros catch. Lucky my eye. The guy ran a mile to get that ball and he didn't shy away from the barrier, did he? Some outfielders might have had an eye on that fence. I've never put much credence in luck anyway. Any athlete who wins relatively consistently is trimming you because he knows how to beat you. A good athlete forces things. If he has a weakness he'll compensate for it, and if you have one he'll exploit it.

Anyway, it's always easy to look at something that's over with, isn't it? Then you can analyze it and say, "This is why it happened."

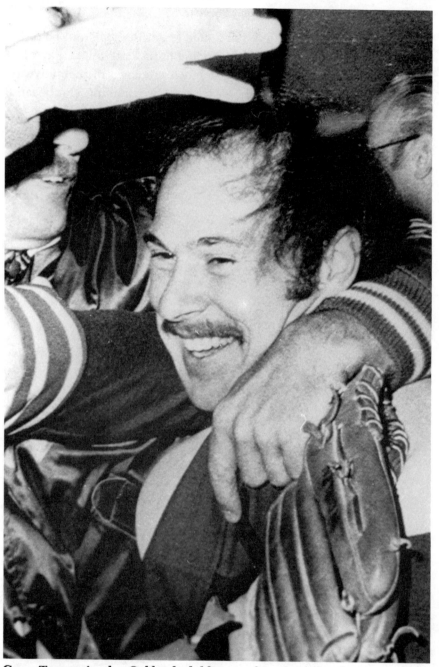

Gene Tenace in the Oakland clubhouse after the seventh game of the 1972 World Series

Gene Tenace

FURY GENE TENACE

Born: October 10, 1946, Russelton, Pennsylvania
Major League career: 1969– Oakland Athletics, San Diego Padres

A versatile, power-hitting ball player, Gene Tenace has been consistently among the league leaders in getting bases on balls, leading the American League in this department in 1974. Tenace, however, will always be remembered as the man who virtually single-handedly tore apart the 1972 World Series. Seldom has a player so completely dominated a Series. His four home runs (hit in the first five games) tied a Series record. Tenace led all hitters in home runs, runs batted in, runs scored, total bases, and posted an incredible .913 slugging average. The most impressive single statistic from that Series, however, is that Gene Tenace drove home nine runs while no other Oakland batter drove in more than one.

IF ANYBODY ever doubts what a strange and unpredictable game baseball is, all you have to do is take out the records of postseason play in 1972 and show it to them. Show them what Gene Tenace did. We played the Tigers in the championship series and it went five games before we finally beat them out. You know what I did in that series? I went 1 for 17 and batted .059. Ten days later I was voted Most Valuable Player in the World Series and my whole career was turned around.

I always wanted to play in the big leagues. My father was a baseball fan, and since I was the only boy in the family he started very early on getting me interested in the game. He wanted me to be a ball player. I was around four years old when he started taking me out for games of catch after dinner. This was in Lucasville, Ohio, where I grew up. We would go outside and just throw the ball back and forth to each other. He was always very patient and encouraging. "That's the way to do it," he would say whenever I threw it straight or whenever I got one in my mitt and was able to hang on to it. And it pleased me no end when he said those things. I guess a boy, any boy, more than anything else wants to impress his father.

I can remember that the World Series was always the big event. When it was on, everything else seemed to come to a standstill. In school they would set up a TV in the all-purpose room and when you had the chance you went in there and watched the game. You just couldn't help it. Baseball is such a long season, you know, and when after all those months and all those games it finally boils down to a few games between the two best teams, it just grips you.

I think the most vivid baseball memory I have from my boyhood years is of Bill Mazeroski's dramatic home run that he hit to win the 1960 Series for the Pirates. If you were a baseball fan that was a tremendous moment, no matter which side you were rooting for. And even though it was always my ambition to be a big league ball player, those kinds of heroics were still a dream, a fantasy world. I mean, winning the seventh game of the World Series with a home run in the bottom of the ninth—how often does it happen? You've got to keep those dreams within bounds, right?

But while I may not have dreamed about doing what Bill Mazeroski did, I sure did dream about playing in a World Series one day myself.

We came close in 1971. We won our division but then lost three straight to Baltimore in the championship series. But we were beginning to put it all together. There was a feeling on that Oakland club that we were going to be there next year.

I didn't really start playing regularly in 1972 until August. Dave Duncan was the first-string catcher most of the year, but then in late July after being in first place for a long time we dropped out and Chicago went past us. Duncan hadn't been hitting too well and it seemed to be affecting his defensive play. So Dick Williams decided to make a move and he put me behind the plate. We got going again after that and moved back into first place and stayed there. I guess

Dick didn't want to break up the combination and he stuck with me for the rest of the year.

I would say that without a doubt that was a crucial point in my career. I'd been sitting around all year not doing much of anything. Under those circumstances, when you feel you should be playing and are not, it's easy to become frustrated and lose interest. But I was lucky. I was rooming with Sal Bando. He wouldn't let me become depressed. He kept telling me day after day to keep ready, to stay in shape and be mentally alert, that an opportunity was going to come. "And when it does come," Sal would say, "you'd better be ready to take advantage of it." This is the type of individual Sal is. He always thinks about other people and that's why he's so valuable to a ball club. He understands your problems, he sympathizes, he cares, and he knows how to communicate. He's one guy you don't judge just by his batting average. One of the luckiest breaks I've ever had in baseball was rooming with Sal Bando for five years.

So when I finally did get the opportunity I was mentally prepared and was able to do the job.

That was the first year we had the mustaches. It began as a promotional thing with Charlie Finley. He said he would give each guy who grew a mustache three hundred dollars. Most everybody went along with it and it became sort of our trademark. In fact, as time went on the mustaches got fancier and the hair got longer. We became known as "The Mustache Gang," and there were a lot of jokes and wisecracks. But we were having the last laugh most of the time because we were winning ball games.

We won the division championship again in '72 and this time played Detroit. The series went the full five and, boy, it got scary. They came into Oakland and we won the first two and I guess we kind of felt we had it wrapped up. But then we went to Detroit and the next thing we know they've won two games and the series is tied. The fourth game was a whistler. It was a 1–1 tie going into the tenth. We scored twice in the top of the tenth and we figured, okay, this is it, we've got them now. But they came back with three in the bottom of the tenth to win it.

That fifth game, which we won, was no bargain either. We beat them 2–1. Vida Blue came in in the sixth inning and turned in a super job.

After that series against Detroit we went into the World Series one very relaxed ball club. We'd been drained. We figured that nothing could be as nerve-wracking as those games.

We were going in against a very strong Cincinnati club and were the underdogs. Reggie Jackson had been hurt in the last game against the Tigers and was out for the Series, which didn't help our chances any.

Cincinnati had a great team, no doubt about it. Tony Perez, Joe Morgan, Bobby Tolan, Pete Rose, Johnny Bench, guys of that caliber. But we knew we had the good pitching and that we'd have a chance if we could stay close. And that's the way it turned out. It was a seven-game Series and six of those games were low-score jobs that were decided by one run.

I'll tell you, catching that staff was a pleasure. I'd have to say that the best pitcher I ever caught was Catfish Hunter. He was great to

Vida Blue. "And he could throw that thing anywhere from 95 to 100 miles an hour."

Pete Rose in 1964

catch because he had such fine control and command of all his pitches. And as good as competitor as you'll ever find.

Vida Blue got by basically on one pitch—his fastball. He had two types of fastball. He could run the ball up and in on you and he could turn it over and make it sink and go away. And he could throw that thing anywhere from ninety-five to a hundred miles an hour.

Ken Holtzman threw the fastball, the good curve, and the change. When he was on he would pretty much go with the fastball and change, always pitching low and away from the batter. Kenny always had a good idea where he wanted to throw the ball. A very intelligent individual.

Rollie Fingers? Well, I would say that through the five years when we had all the success Rollie Fingers was the MVP on our ball club. This guy was just remarkable, coming in day in and day out and consistently doing the job. I can't think of another relief pitcher who has been as consistent year in and year out as Rollie. I'd have to say that with all the great players we had on the Oakland Athletics in those years, and we had some really great ones, to me Rollie Fingers was our most valuable player.

So it was a case of good pitching stopping good hitting. And we also played a great defensive game. Joe Rudi made some memorable catches—remember that one where he climbed the left-field wall?— and Dick Green played an outstanding second base. I don't think our club ever got the credit it deserved for its defensive abilities, but it was solid all around, with a good glove just about everywhere.

As I said, we were pretty relaxed going into the Series. But I'll tell you, all of a sudden I got numb. It was all of those old boyhood dreams coming true. After years and years of reading and talking about the World Series and watching it on television—suddenly I was part of it. And to bring it up even higher for me, the Series opened in Cincinnati, not far from where I lived in Lucasville.

I can tell you exactly when the realization hit me. It was when I came out to the on-deck circle in the first game. I looked around at that big stadium and there were over fifty thousand people there and I knew about all the millions and millions of people around the world who were listening. All of a sudden a blur of memories went through my mind, and one of them was the time some Cincinnati scouts watched me play and said I'd never make it. But mainly I was just plain awestruck, kneeling there and waiting to hit.

The funny thing was, here I was at the height of a professional ball player's career and I was feeling anything but professional. I didn't even feel like a ball player. I felt like a kid. And what it was, I guess, was that kid inside of me, that little boy, that fan, that dreamer, couldn't quite believe what was happening. It's a strange feeling—you set a goal and then you work hard all of your life, you struggle and hustle to make it happen, and then when it does happen you find it hard to believe. I guess in a way this is saying how almost out of reach that goal is to begin with.

And then you become the professional again and realize, hell, just being there isn't enough; you suddenly want to prove that you *belong* there.

You know, when we were going to the park that day on the bus, one of our pitchers, Darold Knowles, said that the Most Valuable Player in the Series was going to be either me or George Hendrick.

I don't know what made him say it, but he actually made that statement. All the guys laughed—and I laughed the loudest.

With two out, George Hendrick walked and I stepped in. Gary Nolan was pitching. Well, my first time at bat I hit one over the left-field wall. It was unbelievable. I had just been trying to make contact. But I'll be darned if it didn't go out. I started around the bases and when I was turning second base I thought I'd look for my folks in the crowd. I knew about where they were sitting, in the third-base boxes. Sure enough, there was my father, jumping up and down and applauding and yelling. With it being a Cincinnati crowd there weren't too many people doing that, and I guess that's how I was able to spot him. I caught his eye and for those few seconds we were looking at each other. It was a great feeling. It isn't often that you hit a home run—in a World Series, no less—and are able to share it like that with just the right person.

And then the next time up—well, if that first one was unbelievable, how do you describe the second one? Gary Nolan threw me a high breaking ball and I really got under it and hit it way up. I just stood there at home plate and watched it rise. I knew it had the distance, it was a question of fair or foul. The ball hung up there for what seemed like a long time, then it all but brushed against the foul pole and went into the second deck.

That's when I started running. When I came around second I looked into the stands and picked out my father again. Well, I thought they were going to have to tie him down. He was jumping higher than the first time, and applauding, and yelling. The whole thing was just unreal. If you saw it in the movies you would say "That's a lot of baloney."

I can't honestly say that when I was coming around second and looking at my father I actually thought back to those days when we used to throw the ball back and forth after dinner and he would say "That's the way to do it," but the emotion of that memory was surely there. For those few seconds it was the two of us alone again, the fifty thousand people weren't there, and he was saying "That's the way to do it," and I was saying "Okay, Dad, I'm getting the hang of it now."

We won that game 3–2. The Cincinnati pitching was tough; we got just four hits off of them, but luckily two of them were my home runs.

We won the next day too, 2–1, behind Catfish Hunter. Joe Rudi hit a home run and then saved the game for us with that spectacular catch against the left-field wall on a drive that Denis Menke hit in the ninth inning.

The clubhouse was pretty lively after that game, as you might imagine. But then Dick Williams came up to me and pulled me aside. He had a very serious look on his face. He told me something that shook me up a little bit: my life had been threatened just before the game. It seems that some guy who was waiting on the ticket line said that if I came close to Babe Ruth's World Series home run record he would kill me. A woman overheard him and reported it to the security guards. They went back with her and she pointed the guy out. They took him out of the line, brought him inside and frisked him. Sure enough he had a loaded pistol on him and a bottle of booze. So they took him away.

Word got down to the clubhouse that my life had been threatened. Everybody knew about it but me. Nobody said anything to me until after the ball game. That's when Dick pulled me aside and told me. He said everything was okay now because they had nabbed the guy. I tried not to let it bother me, but still it gives you a peculiar feeling to hear something like that. I don't suppose I'll ever know what was really in that guy's mind; the fortunate thing is they caught him before he had a chance to do anything.

We left Cincinnati after that game. By the time we returned for the sixth and seventh games I was so wrapped up in the Series I didn't even think about the incident.

Jack Billingham beat us 1–0 in the third game. Johnny Odom pitched well for us but we didn't give him much support. I didn't get any hits that day, nor did I have one in the second game. It looked like I'd come back to earth.

But then in the fourth game I hit another home run, off of Don Gullett this time. He threw me a fastball and I tagged it. Sure I remember the pitch. You don't forget those things. That was in the fifth inning and it gave us a 1–0 lead, which we carried into the top of the eighth. Then Cincinnati scored two runs and we went into the bottom of the ninth down by one.

Well, we came up with a rally. With one out Gonzalo Marquez pinch-hit a single. Then I came up. With a 2–1 count on me they brought in Clay Carroll. Didn't make any difference. I singled to left to put men on first and second. Then Don Mincher pinch-hit a single to tie it up. I went to third. I was standing there with the winning run. Ninety feet away. I can tell you, in a situation like that, home plate is like a magnet trying to pull you in.

Dick Williams sent up another pinch-hitter, Angel Mangual, and darned if he didn't hit one through a drawn-in infield. I came in and jumped on home plate with that winning run. Three pinch-hitters, three base hits. That's some kind of ball club, isn't it?

That put us up three games to one and we were feeling pretty good about things, particularly after that rally.

The next day I hit a three-run homer in the second inning off of Jim McGlothlin. My fourth home run in five games. I wasn't up on my baseball history, so I didn't know I had tied a record until they put it up on the scoreboard that only four other men had ever hit as many home runs in a World Series—Lou Gehrig, Babe Ruth, Duke Snider, and Hank Bauer. When I came back into the dugout, Dick Williams gave me a big hug and I had tears in my eyes, because that's when I finally realized what I had accomplished. It was very emotional for me. Up until that time I had just been trying to play my game and hadn't been paying any attention to records.

It would be nice to say that that home run won the Series for us, but Cincinnati kept coming back one run at a time and finally beat us out, 5–4.

Say, have you been taking notice of those scores?—3–2, 2–1, 1–0, 3–2, 5–4. Five games and you never had a chance to breathe in any of them. But then we just blew out in the next game. They beat us 8–1. That was the only runaway in the whole Series. We were back in Cincinnati then, so that gave their fans something to cheer about.

Gene Tenace hitting his third home run of the Series, against Don Gullett

So it came down to a seventh game. Looking back on it now, I have to say this: when you're hot, you're hot. In the first inning of that game we had a man on third with two out and I hit a ground ball down to third. It hit the seam on the carpet and bounced over Denis Menke's head and scored the run. That's what happened. Everything seemed to be going my way. No matter what they threw up at me I was right on it, and when I needed a bit of luck, I got lucky. Did the Reds start pitching me differently? I'll tell you the truth—I never paid any attention. I was swinging the bat so good it didn't make any difference. I was just locked in, that's all. I was feeling great, seeing the ball good, had my timing just right, and was confident. It didn't seem to matter what they were throwing—fastballs, curves, sliders, changes of speed—I felt I was going to hit it hard somewhere.

It was a completely reverse cycle from the championship series where, after going hitless in the first few games I began to press. I'd say to myself, "You've got to help the ball club," and I started to press. Once you do that you tend to tense up at the plate and break your concentration. That never happened in the World Series. In fact it was just the opposite.

The rally that won it for us occurred in the sixth inning. The game was tied 1–1. Bert Campaneris was on third with two out and I hit a double. Yeah, I was still moving the bat. I went out for a pinch-runner and then Sal Bando hit a double over Bobby Tolan's head and that drove in what proved to be the winning run. The final was 3–2.

I ended up as MVP for the Series and got a car from *Sport* Magazine. After it was over I went back to Lucasville and I guess I was the biggest man in town for a while. They gave me a day there. Even named a ball field after me. Gene Tenace Field, in Lucasville, Ohio.

I would have to say that what I did in the Series that year probably had a big effect on my career. It seemed to make the club believe in me more. That winter they traded Mike Epstein, who had been our regular first baseman, and that gave me an opportunity to play every day. I became the regular first baseman in 1973 and I've been a regular ever since. It all might have happened anyway, even if I hadn't had the good Series; but on the other hand, you can't be sure. One thing, though, is sure: I'll never forget that week in October, 1972.

MONFORD (MONTE) IRVIN
NEGRO LEAGUES 1937-1948
NEW YORK N.L., CHICAGO N.L.,
1949-1956
REGARDED AS ONE OF NEGRO LEAGUES' BEST
HITTERS. STAR SLUGGER OF NEWARK EAGLES
WON 1946 NEGRO LEAGUE BATTING TITLE.
LED N.L. IN RUNS BATTED IN AND PACED
"MIRACLE" GIANTS IN HITTING IN 1951
DRIVE TO PENNANT. BATTED .458 AND
STOLE HOME IN 1951 WORLD SERIES.

Monte Irvin Hall of Fame plaque

Monte Irvin

OF COURSE the highlight of any ball player's life is the World Series. This is what you dream about when you're a youngster, what you look forward to and strive for as a player, what you get in shape for in spring training, and why you play a long hard schedule. Well, finally in 1951 I was getting to play in a World Series. The dream come true, the payoff for all the struggle and the hard work, the highlight of your professional life—and the whole thing seemed anti-climactic. No matter what happened in the Series, it wasn't going to top the drama and the excitement and the emotional pitch of what had happened the day before.

I've said on a number of occasions that I cannot conceive of my life without 1951, that pennant race, that playoff, that home run. I think every player who has any sort of career at all should have a moment like the moment we had in 1951, when we came from no-where to catch the Dodgers on the last day and then beat them in the playoff. And not only did we beat them but we did it so dramatically, when Bobby Thomson did the unexpected, on October 3, 1951.

Recently Hank Aaron's 715th home run was selected as the most memorable moment in baseball history. Well, we knew after Hank Aaron had hit his 714th home run that it was just a matter of time before he hit the record breaker. But Bobby's feat was totally unex-pected, it was sudden and stunning, came under the greatest pressure imaginable, and was the most unbelievable experience for everyone connected with it.

That was one time when the pennant winners didn't pour the champagne all over each other. No sir—we drank it. We needed it. We were just so emotionally exhausted. The pandemonium in that clubhouse was incredible. You see, all the TV cameras and everything else had been set up in the Dodger clubhouse, in anticipation of Brooklyn holding that lead in the bottom of the ninth. Well, when Bobby hit the home run it started a mad scramble from one clubhouse to the other. I remember Don Newcombe telling me later that they almost knocked him over with a camera in their haste to get over to our clubhouse. And just a moment before, Newk was waiting to be interviewed as the winning pitcher.

We took our time getting out of the clubhouse and it was starting to get dark out when I drove home. I was still on an emotional high and I can remember suddenly thinking, *Hey, tomorrow I've got to play in a World Series.*

I would have preferred a few days off, which you always do get, to have a chance to savor the victory. Also I wanted some time to think about the Yankees, about their pitchers, about how to play certain hitters. But we didn't have that luxury. Another factor—and this was more serious—was that our pitchers were worn out from the playoff. Sal Maglie, Larry Jansen and Jim Hearn had all worked.

Nevertheless, we were good and loose when we got together at

Larry Jansen

Monte Irvin

Yankee Stadium the next day. What had happened the day before had taken all the pressure off. We were probably the most relaxed team ever to go into a World Series. Hell, less than twenty-four hours before we had just about given up hope.

Leo didn't hold a meeting when we got together. All he told us was to keep on playing the way we had been, that we were doing just fine. Durocher was an inspired manager that year. He kept making the most astounding moves and seeing them pay off. Things like the right pinch-hitter at the right time, the right pitching change at the right time, moving his fielders around. It seemed that over the last few months of the season he just couldn't make a wrong move.

There's a theory about Leo, to the effect that when he's got a winning team and he's in the race there is no better manager, and that when he's out of contention he tends to lose interest. I would agree with that, to a certain extent. In 1951 we saw his managerial genius in all its glory.

He was the kind of manager who absolutely could not tolerate mediocrity. He expected and demanded the most that you could give. If you didn't hustle you couldn't play for him. He would get on you and if you couldn't take it he'd ride you right off the ball club. He could get pretty rough. Sometimes he didn't have the patience to groom a young player. But he handled Willie Mays just perfectly. He knew just when to give Willie the pat on the back, and occasionally when Willie got the winning hit Leo would take him out and buy him a new suit of clothes or a half-dozen shirts. Willie developed a great trust in Leo and depended on him a lot for advice, on the field and off.

But we just weren't psychologically ready for a World Series, and I guess you would have to say it was understandable. It was a completely different attitude from the one we had three years later, in 1954, when we played Cleveland.

People have called that one of the biggest surprises in World Series history, because after Cleveland won 111 games in the regular season, we ran over them in four straight. Well, we weren't surprised at all. We were very confident, because we used to play them in the spring and beat them regularly. They had good power and outstanding pitching, but their defense wasn't too good and they didn't have much speed. So in spite of those fine pitchers—Early Wynn, Bob Lemon, Mike Garcia, Bob Feller, Art Houtteman, Ray Narleski, Don Mossi—and in spite of their 111 wins, we were confident.

We had the kind of hitters who could move the ball around, fellows like Al Dark, Whitey Lockman, Don Mueller, in addition to Henry Thompson and myself, and Willie was a full-fledged star by that time. That famous catch he made on Vic Wertz helped to break Cleveland's back, and so did those pinch-hits by Dusty Rhodes. We had enough pitching too. Sal Maglie, Hoyt Wilhelm, Ruben Gomez, and Johnny Antonelli. Johnny was our ace that year. He could throw so hard he was simply overpowering.

Just to show you how Durocher played that Series, we had beaten them three straight and were ahead in the fourth game 7–4 in the eighth inning when the Indians got a couple of men on base. Do

Cleveland's four aces in 1954. Left to right, Mike Garcia, Early Wynn, Bob Feller, and Bob Lemon

you know who Leo brought in to relieve in that spot? Antonelli. That's right. His ace. Johnny had pitched nine innings just two days before, but Leo smelled four straight and he wanted it. He had them down and wanted to keep them down. Johnny came in, faced five men, got three strikeouts and two pop-ups and that was it. Four straight.

That was 1954. It was different in 1951. As I said, we weren't psychologically ready for a World Series. Nevertheless we played good ball and gave the Yankees a run for it. I got off to a particularly strong start with hits my first four times up, and all of them against one of the toughest right-handed pitchers in the game—Allie Reynolds.

My first time up we had a man on first and two out. I singled to right-center. Then Whitey Lockman followed with a double, scoring one run and sending me to third.

While I was standing on third I noticed that Reynolds was taking a long time to deliver the ball. He was ducking his head and looking down as he went into his motion. Now, I had stolen home five times during the regular season. A lot of people don't know that. I called Leo over from the coaching box and said, "Leo, I think I can make it."

"All right," he said. "Take a good lead. If you think you've got the jump, go ahead. It's two out anyhow."

Bobby Thomson was the batter and I was lucky because he was alert up there. I took off on the next pitch, steaming for home plate. When Bobby saw me coming he hung in there just long enough to block Berra's vision and then fell back. What enabled me to get in there safely, I think, was that the pitch was high and Yogi had to reach up for it and then bring his glove down. If the pitch had been low I don't think I would have made it. It was very close, but I slid in under the tag. When the umpire called me safe, Yogi jumped up and yelled, "No, no, no!"

I said, "Yogi, yes, yes, yes."

He looked at me and said, "What are you talking about?"

"That's what it's going to say in the papers tomorrow: Yes."

And you know, the pictures showed the next day that I was clearly in there. Yogi came up to me before the second game and admitted it.

So I had that single in the first, and then another single in the third, and in the fifth I tripled over DiMaggio's head in center, and in the sixth another single. Four for four.

I didn't realize it at the time, but nobody had ever gone five for five in a World Series game. They still haven't. Somebody's got to set that record soon. I came up again in the eighth inning. As I stepped into the box Yogi said, "Monte, you're hitting everything. Curves, fastballs; high, low, in between. I don't know what to throw you."

I just laughed. Then he said, "I think I'll tell him to just wind up and throw it right down the middle."

Well, I knew Yogi was good for talking to a hitter, and anyway, I knew enough never to believe what a catcher tells you. So I paid no attention. I stepped in and lo and behold—Yogi was telling the truth. I saw this fastball coming right over the heart of the plate. I was so surprised that I swung late and hit a line drive right into Joe Collins' glove at first. I whacked the ball real well and another few inches either way and I would have had that hit. I've always been sorry I didn't get it. I came close, but coming close doesn't make a story, does it?

We won that game, 5–1. Dave Koslo started for us and he went all the way. As I mentioned before, we were hurting for pitchers and Leo had to reach far down into the staff for Koslo. But Dave was always a good pitcher and he worked a strong game that day.

In the second game we started Larry Jansen against Eddie Lopat. Lopat had a style completely different from Reynolds'. Allie threw that fire, while Eddie threw what they called "junk." Some junk! It was a beautiful variety of breaking balls and changes of speeds. And then when he did come in with his fast one, you weren't ready for it. He was tough that day, very tough. Jansen pitched well but Lopat was better and beat us, 3–1.

Lopat gave us only five hits, but I was still in my groove and got three of them. I got seven hits my first nine times up. I stole a base, too, in that game. There was something I never realized until it was pointed out to me later, some time after the Series. My two steals were the only ones in the entire Series. Nobody else stole a base.

What were they throwing me? Tell you the truth, I didn't know and didn't care. That's the way it is when you're in that groove and hitting the ball. It makes no difference what's coming in at you—high or low, fast or slow. You just rap it out.

My power was to right-center, but I was hitting balls all over the place in that Series. A lot of people have always felt that I was at a disadvantage playing in the Polo Grounds, with those deep power alleys. There was many a 450-foot drive I hit there that dropped into an outfielder's glove. A park like Ebbets Field, with those short fences,

Monte Irvin stealing home in the first game of the 1951 World Series. The batter is Bobby Thomson, the catcher Yogi Berra, the umpire Bill Summers

Willie Mays with Minneapolis in 1951

might have been better for me. I tend to agree with that, but on the other hand, some people feel if you're a .250 hitter, you're going to hit .250 wherever you are, and if you're a .300 hitter, you're going to hit .300 no matter where you play. And, too, maybe they would have pitched me differently if I had played in Ebbets Field. There are any number of ways to look at it. For instance, in the Polo Grounds they didn't like to pitch me inside because of the short fences down the line, so in a way they were almost obligated to pitch into my power. So maybe I was better off playing there, even though that ball park sure could break your heart sometimes.

You know, there was a play in that second game that was of some interest, especially if you like to think about baseball history, which I do. It happened in the fifth inning. Let me set it up for you. That was Willie Mays' first World Series and Mickey Mantle's first World Series—they were both rookies that year—and it was Joe DiMaggio's last World Series. Joe retired a few weeks later. I guess you might say that Series saw a changing of the guard, the great center fielder of the past going out and the two great center fielders of the future coming in, all on the same field at the same time.

Mickey, of course, was playing right field. Well, a ball was hit to right-center in the fifth inning. Joe and Mickey went for it and at the last minute Mickey lay back and let Joe take it. But in doing so, Mantle stepped on something in the outfield—I think it was a loose drainage cap—and went down like he'd been shot. He hurt his knee badly and had to be taken out of the game. He didn't play again in the Series. That was a bad injury, one of several that I believe bothered him throughout his career and impaired his effectiveness. And do you know who hit that fly ball? It was Willie.

I had great admiration for DiMaggio. We all did. It used to amaze me how graceful he was in the outfield, how stylish he was in going after a ball. He never seemed to be in a hurry, but yet he was always there. And we admired that classic batting stance of his, with the bat held high and the fact that he didn't stride very much, just lifted that left foot up and put it down four or five inches ahead. You couldn't fool him with a change-up, he was always ready for a curve, and you couldn't throw the fast one by him.

It's hard to compare him with Willie because Joe was past his prime in that Series. But I guess you would have to credit them with being the two greatest center fielders of modern times. Their styles out there were so dissimilar. Joe was smooth, Willie was always running out from under his cap, making basket catches, diving after balls. He may not have looked as graceful as Joe, but he made every play, and a lot of them were plays that nobody ever expected him to make. Like that catch on Vic Wertz in the 1954 Series. It was one of the greatest catches I've ever seen. He's tried to play that one down. I didn't think he had a chance in the world to get even near that ball, but yet he told me he had it all the way. His judgment was that precise.

We went back to the Polo Grounds for the third game. Jim Hearn pitched a strong game for us and we beat Vic Raschi, never an easy thing to do. The score was 6–2. We broke it open with a five-run rally in the bottom of the fifth inning. There was a very controversial play in that inning, one that still gets some comment now and then, especially from Phil Rizzuto, the Yankee shortstop.

With one out, Eddie Stanky walked. Then he attempted to steal second. Berra's throw was on the money and in plenty of time. Rizzuto had the ball in his glove waiting. Well, what Eddie did—as you know he was a very aggressive player—was put his foot right into the glove and kick the ball out. The ball rolled into the outfield and Eddie got up and went to third. That opened the door. A couple of base hits followed and then Whitey Lockman lined a home run.

But that play still stands out. Because it happened in a World Series and was the turning point of a game, people will always remember it. Rizzuto thought it was dirty baseball and never forgave Stanky for doing it. I understand that to this day Phil is still sore about it and that the air turns a bit chilly whenever those two fellows meet. But that was the way Stanky played ball. What I think must have happened was that Phil, as good a shortstop as he was, wasn't clutching the ball securely enough. I guess he thought it was going to be a routine out and was letting the ball lie in an open glove rather than squeezing it. To add insult to injury, Rizzuto was given an error on the play. All five runs in that inning were unearned.

So now we were up two games to one and were looking forward to going all the way. But then we got a bad break. You see, there was no off day between games, and the Yankees had but the three starting pitchers—Reynolds, Lopat, Raschi. So they were going to pitch a rookie, Tom Morgan, in the fourth game. Morgan was a pretty good pitcher but we thought we'd be able to hit him. But then it rained. It just poured. The game was called, Reynolds had an extra day of rest and he came back to pitch the fourth game. Our fortunes went downhill from that point.

Reynolds beat us, 6–2. I got two more hits, but that didn't make me feel too good. I felt better in the third game, when I didn't get any hits and we won.

The fifth game was a shambles for us. The Yankees simply erupted. They beat us 13–1. Gil McDougald hit a grand slam home run. Lopat beat us again. Eddie pitched brilliantly in that Series. I think we got only one earned run off of him in two games.

I got my 10th and 11th hits in that game. And I almost had another. I came up in the bottom of the ninth and really caught hold of one. Hardest ball I hit all Series. It went out to left-center like a shot. As I started running I figured it was going to be in for a triple or maybe even an inside-the-park homer. At the last second Gene Woodling came from nowhere in left field and dove through the air and caught the ball as he was landing on his belly. What a great catch he made. It deprived me of setting a new record for hits in a six-game Series. It just goes to show you how baseball is played. It was the bottom of the ninth and we're losing 13–1, but yet Gene was ready to break his neck to get that ball. And of course that's the way it should be played.

I kidded Gene about it after the Series.

"You cost me a record," I told him. "The score is 13–1 and you nearly kill yourself to beat me out of a hit."

"You should have told me," he said.

"Told you what?"

"That you needed it for a record."

"You would have let it drop?" I asked.

"Sure," he said.

"Like hell," I said.

He laughed like anything. He was a great kidder. No way would he let a ball drop. The score could have been 50–1 and he would have done the same thing. Heck of a ballplayer, Gene Woodling.

So we were down three games to two and moving back to Yankee Stadium. Koslo started for us and Raschi for them. We hated to see Vic out there; he was a very tough pitcher and never more so than in these situations.

Koslo pitched all right until the bottom of the sixth. It was tied 1–1 to that point. Then the Yankees loaded the bases with two out. Hank Bauer was the batter. He tied into one and hit it out to left field, where I was playing. I didn't think he could hit a ball that far. It just plain took off and went over my head. It hit the fence and rattled around. I think Willie finally picked it up and threw it back in. Three runs scored and Bauer got a triple. That was the big hit.

We were losing 4–1 in the top of the ninth and gave it one more shot. The first three men up got hits and the bases were loaded with none out. It looked like maybe we had another miracle brewing.

Stengel brought in a left-hander, Bob Kuzava, to pitch to three right-handed hitters—me, Bobby Thomson, and Sal Yvars, who came on to pinch-hit. That looked unorthodox, but the reason was Kuzava could get right-handed hitters out better than he could lefties. He threw a sinking fastball that was rough on righties. But still, it was a risky move. I once asked Stengel about it, later on. He tapped his finger against his forehead and said, "Smart. The old man knows. The old man is smart."

Smart, no doubt about it, but a little bit lucky too that day, because we hit Kuzava hard. I hit a long fly ball to left field that was deep enough to advance all the runners. Then Bobby hit one out to left field even farther. If we had been in the Polo Grounds it would have been a home run and Bobby would have been a hero all over again. But it was caught. The runners moved up again. That left a man on third, two out and the score 4–3.

Leo sent Sal Yvars up to bat for Henry Thompson. We were sitting on the bench wondering if we had any more miracles left in our bag. And for a second we thought we did. Sal really ripped one. He sent

Bobby Thomson in Phoenix, spring of 1952

a screaming line drive out to right field. Hank Bauer went rushing for it and as he did he lost his footing. He slipped and fell, but somehow he caught the ball and held onto it. It was a hell of a catch.

That ended the Series. You hate to see it end like that—with the tying run crossing the plate just as the outfielder is falling down and making a sensational grab of a sizzling line drive.

But I'll tell you the truth, as much as we wanted to win the Series, we didn't feel that badly let down. We were still thinking about the playoff against the Dodgers. That was our year, right there, when Bobby hit that ball.

Les Bell in 1930

Les Bell

LESTER ROWLAND BELL

Born: December 14, 1901, Harrisburg, Pennsylvania
Major League career: 1923–1931, St. Louis Cardinals, Boston Braves, Chicago Cubs
Lifetime average: .290

Playing with steady, quiet efficiency, Les Bell was one of the National League's better third basemen in the 1920's. His finest year was 1926, when the Cardinals won their first pennant and went on to defeat the Yankees in the World Series. Bell batted .325 that year, drove home 100 runs, hit 17 home runs, and played an excellent third base.

I CAN see him yet, to this day, walking in from the left-field bull pen through the gray mist. The Yankee fans recognized him right off, of course, but you didn't hear a sound from anywhere in that stadium. They just sat there and watched him walk in. And he took his time. Grover Cleveland Alexander was never in a hurry, and especially not this day. It was the seventh game of the World Series, he had pitched nine innings the day before, and he was coming in now to face a tough young hitter with two out and the bases loaded. It was the bottom of the seventh inning and the score was 3–2 in our favor.

Yeah, I can still see him walking that long distance. He just came straggling along, a lean old Nebraskan, wearing a Cardinal sweater, his face wrinkled, that cap sitting on top of his head and tilted to one side—that's the way he liked to wear it.

We were all standing on the mound waiting for him—me and Rogers Hornsby (who was our manager and second baseman) and Tommy Thevenow and Jim Bottomley and Bob O'Farrell. When Alec reached the mound, Rog handed him the ball and said, "There's two

83

out and they're drunk"—meaning the bases were loaded—"and Lazzeri's the hitter."

"Okay," Alec said. "I'll tell you what I'm gonna do. I'm gonna throw the first one inside to him. Fast."

"No, no," Rog said. "You can't do that."

Alec nodded his head very patiently and said, "Yes I can. Because if I do and he swings at it he'll most likely hit it on the handle, or if he does hit it good it'll go foul. Then I'm going to come outside with my breaking pitch."

Rog looked him over for a moment, then gave Alec a slow smile and said, "Who am I to tell *you* how to pitch?"

Then, to show you what kind of pitcher Alec was and what kind of thinking he did out there, he said, "I've got to get Lazzeri out. Then in the eighth inning I've got to get Dugan, I've got to get Collins, and I've got to get Pennock or whoever hits for him, one, two, three. Then in the ninth I've got to get Combs and I've got to get Koenig, one, two, so when that big son of a bitch comes up there"—meaning Ruth, of course—"the best he can do is tie the ball game." He had it figured out that Ruth was going to be the last hitter in the ninth inning.

So we all went back to our positions—I was playing third base—and Alec got set to work. He had gone nine the day before, and if he got out of this jam he still had two more innings to go today, he was nearly forty years old—but doggone, there wasn't another man in the world I would have rather seen out there at that moment than Grover Cleveland Alexander.

The first time I ever saw Grover Cleveland Alexander was in 1915. I was thirteen years old at the time. My Dad, who worked for the railroad, got a pass and took me from Harrisburg to Philadelphia to see a big league game for the first time. We saw the Phillies play at Baker Bowl. Boy, that was a big day in my life. Alec didn't pitch that day, but I saw him throwing on the sidelines. Couldn't keep my eyes off him. Another player I remember seeing was Gavvy Cravath—he was the champion home run hitter at that time. When I got back home I was the center of attention—none of my friends had ever seen

Sgt. Grover Cleveland Alexander in 1918

a big league game and they wanted to hear all about it. The next big league game I saw was eight years later, in 1923, when I was in the lineup for the Cardinals.

I was born and raised in Harrisburg. It was great growing up there in those years. Harrisburg was really a nice place. It was the capital city and it was a railroad town, the division point for the Pennsylvania Railroad between New York and Chicago and St. Louis. My Dad was a railroader all his life, a freight conductor, working in the yards in Harrisburg. When I came out of high school he said to me, "If you get a job on the railroad, I'll have you fired." Railroading was a tough job in those days, real tough. So it was the old story of a father wanting to see his son do better than he did. But I told him he didn't have to worry—I had my sights set on playing ball.

I was crazy about baseball. Always played it, as far back as I can remember. It was all I ever wanted to do. We always had a little pick-up team going. We'd get hold of gloves somehow—usually hand-me-downs—and we would make our own baseballs. We would take a little rubber ball and wrap twine around it and put friction tape on the outside. That's how it was done. And the darn thing would last a little while, too.

I went into semipro ball in 1919, after graduating high school. In those days semipro was a very good brand of ball around Harrisburg, and well organized. I played a few games a week in Harrisburg and

Gavvy Cravath in 1915. "He was the champion home run hitter at that time."

then a few games in a little town called Columbia, not too far from Lancaster. All told I was making around seventy dollars a week playing semipro, which was decent money in those days.

Our manager in Columbia was Jimmy Sheckard, the old Cub outfielder. One day he said to me, "You interested in playing pro ball?" I told him I sure was. So he had a scout come in and look me over, a fellow named Billy Doyle from the Detroit Tigers. Doyle had his look and signed me and sent me down to Bristol, Tennessee. The funny thing was, I signed for two hundred dollars a month—less money than I was making in semipro. But that didn't bother me; I wanted a crack at pro ball. Sometimes you just feel that you've got to stretch yourself, see how good you are, and money is of secondary importance. I told myself I'd give it four years at most to see if I could make it to the major leagues, and if I couldn't, then I'd come back home and go to work.

Well, I went down to Bristol, stayed two weeks and got fired. Never did know why. The manager's name was Bell too, so maybe he figured one Bell on the club was enough.

When I got back home, Billy Doyle wrote me a letter and said not to worry, he would find me a job the next year. Which he did. Sent me out to Lansing, Michigan, in the Central League. I had no problems out there, played the whole season and hit .329. In the middle of the season the Cardinals bought me. They moved me around, to Syracuse, Houston, then to Milwaukee. In '23 they brought me up for a few games at the tail end of the season.

I'll never forget my first big league game. The club wasn't going anywhere, so they loaded the lineup with kids, me at third, another fellow at first, and so on. The first ball that was hit down to me I picked up cleanly and threw with everything I had. Listen, I had a strong arm. I sure did. I think I must have broken a seat ten or fifteen rows behind first base with that throw. A couple of innings later I had my second chance. This time that ball really flew, and I must have broken a seat *twenty* rows behind first base. When I came into the dugout after that inning I was feeling pretty blue. Who sits down next to me but the regular first baseman, Jim Bottomley. All he did that year was hit .371.

Babe Ruth

Jim Bottomley. "What a fine gentleman he was, and a great ball player."

Jim put his arm around me and said, "Now, kid, Old Jim will be out there tomorrow playing first base. So when you throw the ball, just throw it in the *direction* of the base and Old Jim will get it."

That made me feel better, but I got to laugh now when I think of it. I was twenty-one and "Old Jim" was all of twenty-three. They called him "Sunny Jim" and he sure was all of that. What a fine gentleman he was, and a great ball player. He could do it all.

In 1924 I had a whale of a year with Milwaukee in the American Association, hitting .365. By that time I knew I could make the big leagues. I was itching for it. You can't hardly believe what a feeling it is when you know you're ready to bust out. In '25 I joined the Cardinals and became their regular third baseman.

I loved playing in the big leagues. Boy, I just loved it. It was everything I dreamed it would be and then some. What a way to make a living! I even enjoyed those long train rides, swinging back and forth across the country. I'd sit by the window and watch the farmland and small towns pass by, and now and then see a Model-T tooling along the country roads. You didn't see too many cars back then, especially in the boondocks.

The biggest day I ever had on a ball field was June 2, 1928, when I was with the Braves. We were playing Cincinnati at home and I hit three home runs in one game and came darned near a fourth. There was a screen that ran along the left field bleachers and stopped at an iron pole in center field. I hit a ball out there and it just hit that pole at the edge of the screen and ricocheted out into right-center. I got a triple out of it but had just missed another home run. I would have been the first man since Ed Delahanty in 1896 to hit four in one game. The funny thing about it was, I wasn't a home-run hitter; in fact that year I hit only ten. But I did get three of them in one game. It was a Saturday afternoon and the next morning I went out and bought every Sunday paper in Boston.

I had been traded to the Braves in 1928. We had an awful team. Just awful. In 1929 the owner of the ball club, Judge Fuchs, decided he would manage. I guess he figured it was an easy job and that he could save a few bucks by not having to pay a manager. In a sense it was an easy job; all you had to know was how to lose. John Mc-Graw, Joe McCarthy and Connie Mack working together couldn't have done anything with that team. The Judge didn't know a thing about baseball, and he would sit on the bench and talk to the boys about one thing or another, not paying too much mind to what was going on out on the field. But he was a swell guy and the boys liked him. I remember one time Johnny Evers, who was one of our coaches, said to the Judge that the count was three and one on our batter and what did the Judge want the man to do.

"Tell him to hit a home run," the Judge said.

The year before, in '28, Hornsby was there, playing and managing. He led the league that year with .387. Paul Waner was chasing him most of the summer—I think Paul ended up around .370 or so. Anyway, toward the end of the year Pittsburgh came in for a series and the batting race was pretty close at the time. The papers made a big fuss over "The Battle for the Batting Championship." There wasn't much else to fuss over. Rog really went to town and got a carload of hits in the series while Waner didn't do too well. When it was over, Paul and Hornsby happened to be going back together through the runway underneath the stands to the clubhouses.

"Well, Rog," Paul said, "it looks like you're gonna beat me."

Rog scowled at him and said, "You didn't doubt for a minute that I would, did you?"

Hornsby was the greatest right-handed hitter that ever lived, I can guarantee you that. Maybe even the greatest hitter, period. He had the finest coordination I ever saw. And confidence. He had that by the ton. He just didn't think anybody could get him out. And damned few could. He was a picture up there. So rhythmic. He used a heavy bat —38 ounces and even heavier in the spring—and he held it back and up and he stepped into that ball so easily, from way back in the box. Everything so smooth. I copied him. They used to call me a pup out of Hornsby. I did all right, but nobody could hit like Rog.

Funny thing, I played for three different teams—the Cardinals, Braves and Cubs—and on each one, at one time or another, Hornsby was the manager. It got so that when I saw Rog starting to pack his bags I'd reach for mine.

I've heard a lot of ball players say he was a tough man to play for. I never found him that way. All he ever asked of anybody was that they give him all they had out on the field. "You're only out there for a couple of hours," he would say. Well, I don't think he was asking too much. Yes, I got along with him fine, wherever I played for him.

He was a lone wolf, you know. Even as a player, he never roomed with anybody. And you would never see him anywhere, outside of the hotel lobby. He wouldn't go to the movies because he said it was bad for the eyes. And about the only thing he would read was the racing form because he said reading was bad for the eyes too. Was he neurotic about his eyesight? Well, maybe he was. But there was that stretch over five years where he averaged around .400. So maybe Rog knew what he was doing.

There was another thing that Hornsby could do that a lot of people don't realize—he could run. When he was stretching out on a triple, he was a sight to see. If he had hit left-handed he probably would have hit .450. He was a streak going down that line. And you know, that infield in St. Louis cost him a lot of hits. Around the Fourth of July it had been baked out to concrete, and Rog always hit bullets— he seldom put his bat on the ball that it didn't whistle off. On that infield, those ground balls were in the infielder's glove in no time.

In 1926 we went to spring training in San Antonio. Hornsby was never much of a guy for holding meetings, but he held one on the first day of spring training. I'll never forget it.

"If there's anybody in this room who doesn't think we're going to win the pennant," he said, "go upstairs now and get your money and go on home, because we don't want you around here."

That's the attitude we all started with, right from the first day of spring training. And it carried us all the way, to the pennant, to the World Championship. And for me, personally, it was a great year. I hit .325, knocked in one hundred runs, was up among the league leaders in a lot of departments. I even outhit Rog that year, believe it or not—that was the only time over a ten-year stretch that he was under .360. Yeah, when I think of baseball, I think of 1926.

We won a very close pennant race that year. Beat out Cincinnati by two games. We finished up in the east, in the Polo Grounds. We opened up there on a Thursday and Cincinnati was playing in Phila-delphia. All we needed was one win or one Cincinnati loss to clinch it. We kept watching the scoreboard all afternoon. I think we must have paid more attention to the Red–Phillie game than to our own. Anyway, we lost and the Reds won. So we still needed that one game. The next day we played the Giants again, but there was no score showing up for Cincinnati and Philadelphia. We figured they had been rained out. Well, we won, and then found out later that Hornsby had felt we had been too distracted by the scoreboard and he asked that no Cincinnati score be shown until our game was over. Sure ball players watch the scoreboard in a close pennant race. Don't think they don't.

I'll never forget what a thrill it was walking into Yankee Stadium for the first time, on the opening day of the '26 Series. That ball park was up for only a few years at that time but already there was a magic about it. It was big and beautiful and *important*-looking. And of course Babe Ruth played there. Maybe that was it: Babe Ruth.

I'd never seen so many people in my life—there were over 60,000 packed in there. In those days you had to come out through the Yankee dugout to get over to your own, and I guess when I walked onto the field and saw all those people I must have started shaking. Bill Sherdel, our little left-hander, put his arm around my shoulder and he calmed me down by saying, "Hey, Les, I'll tell you what to do."

"What's that, Bill?" I asked.

"You count 'em upstairs and I'll count 'em downstairs and we'll see how much money we're gonna make today."

I think a lot of people underestimated our ball club in that Series. The Yankees were top-heavy favorites. They had a great team with Ruth, Lou Gehrig, Earle Combs, Bob Meusel, Tony Lazzeri, Joe Dugan, Mark Koenig. And some first-rate pitchers in Herb Pennock, Waite Hoyt, Urban Shocker, Bob Shawkey. But we were fired up and we nearly won that doggone first game. Sherdel pitched beauti-fully but Pennock was a little bit better and beat us, 2–1.

Alexander got us even the next day, 6–2. Billy Southworth hit a home run with two on in the seventh and that was the clincher. Alec

Earle Combs

had them beating it in the dirt all day. I don't think there was more than one putout in our outfield. Alec was really on his game that day. When he was pitching like that the outfielders might just as well have set up a card table out there and played pinochle, for all they had to do.

You know, I was shut out those first two games. Went nothing for seven. Didn't get my first hit until we went back to St. Louis for the third game.

Man, what a parade they had waiting for us when we got back! You see, we had played most of our September schedule on the road and this was the first time we were back home in almost four weeks. So right in the middle of the World Series, St. Louis turned out for us, to celebrate the winning of the pennant. It was no ordinary pennant, you understand—it was the first ever for St. Louis. The Browns had never won one and neither had the Cardinals.

The train pulled in around three o'clock in the afternoon and they had a line of open touring cars waiting for us. We piled into the cars and they had this parade along Olive Street through downtown St. Louis. The streets were so packed there was just room enough for the cars to get through. Everybody was cheering and yelling and the ticker tape was pouring down like a blizzard. Why, we had trouble getting out of those automobiles into the hotel, what with everybody crowding around wanting to pat us on the back and shake our hands.

The next day Jess Haines started for us against Dutch Ruether. It was no score going into the bottom of the fourth. Then I started the inning off with my first hit of the Series, a single over second. Bob O'Farrell walked. Then there was an error in the infield on a double play ball that Tommy Thevenow hit to Lazzeri. Lazzeri flipped it to Koenig but Koenig's throw to first was wild and I scored the first run. Then Jess Haines, of all people, hit a home run into the right-field bleachers. He went on from there to shut them out, 4–0.

I'll tell you a funny story about that game. We scored those three runs in the fourth inning. Okay. Well, the inning before, Haines had led off with a hit and he got around to third base with one out and Hornsby and Bottomley coming up. Pretty good spot, wouldn't you think? But neither one of them could get him in. Now, there was a jewelry store in St. Louis that had put up as a prize a pocket watch for whoever scored the first Cardinal run in St. Louis. It was a beauty of a watch, too, with a baseball on it surrounded by diamonds. So there was old Jess standing on third with one out and Hornsby and Bottomley the hitters. Jess said later he could just feel that watch in the palm of his hand. But they never got him in. Then an inning later I score the first run. So I got the watch, and every time I showed it to Haines he would scowl and say, "Yeah, that ought to be mine."

The fourth game belonged to the Babe. No question about it. He was something to watch that day. What a show!

Flint Rhem started for us. Do you know about Flint? Well, he came from a well-to-do family down in South Carolina. As a matter of fact, I think the town was even named for his family: Rhems, South Carolina. Flint was Alexander's drinking buddy, which meant he had to be pretty good. One time we had a couple of off-days between Pittsburgh and Boston and Rog sent Flint and Alec to New York to rest up there and wait for the club to come in. Well, those two guys went on a binge that was unbelievable. When we pulled into New York, Flint, in particular, was so gassed up he could hardly see. When he sobered up, his explanation was a beauty: he said he didn't want Alec to get drunk, so he had kept drinking all the whiskey around them just to keep it away from Alec.

Flint won twenty games for us that year, but all the same it was a mistake to start him in the Series. In fact, Bill Killefer, one of our coaches, begged Hornsby not to do it.

"The Yankees will murder him," Bill said.

"Maybe," Rog said. "But he won for me all year. I'm a game up and I can afford to take the chance. He's earned it."

Flint's control wasn't that good, you see. You had to have control to pitch against the Yankees, otherwise they'd kill you, I don't care who you were. To give you an example, Flint started off the game by striking out Combs and Koenig. Then he got Ruth two quick strikes

Left to right, Billy Southworth, Taylor Douthit, and Chick Hafey, in 1926

and decided he would throw the next one right on by Babe. Well, you couldn't pitch Ruth like that. He hit that ball over the doggone pavilion. Next time up he hit one out even farther. Then in the sixth inning—Flint was gone by this time—he hit the granddaddy of them all. He hit one out to center field that Taylor Douthit started in on. But that ball just kept rising and rising and ended by ricocheting in the top row of the center-field bleachers, 485 feet away. If the bleachers hadn't been there, I think that ball would have torn down the YMCA building across the street.

They thumped us good, 10–5.

Then we lost the fifth game in ten innings, 3–2. We should have won that son of a buck in nine. We were leading 2–1 going into the top of the ninth. Gehrig led off with a little Texas League double into left-center that just fell away from Thevenow, Wattie Holm and Hafey. Lou eventually came around to tie it and they went on to win it in the tenth.

So we went back to New York, down three games to two, and there were a lot of people who wouldn't have given a plugged nickel for our chances. We were going to have to win two games in that big Yankee Stadium.

When we got into New York we saw in the papers that Miller Huggins was going to start Bob Shawkey. Bob was a good pitcher, but we figured we could hit him, and we did. Started right off in the first inning. We scored one run and had men on second and third and I lined a hit over Joe Dugan's head to score them. Alec was pitching and we were never headed. It was still fairly close going into the seventh, 4–1. We scored a few more and then I came up against Urban Shocker. I caught one and hit it into the left-field bleachers. That was the icing. Alec kept tooling right along and we won it by 10–2.

I'll tell you something else about that Ruth. He could throw. In the ninth inning I lined a hit into right-center. I figured I could get two out of it because Ruth had to go to his right and then turn around to throw. I thought it was a cinch double, but he came around and fired a strike right in there on one hop and got me. It came in with a zing, too. I had heard that you didn't take liberties with his arm, but there's always that little space between hearing something and believing it, and sometimes you just have to have it filled in for you, don't you?

So now it was all tied, three games apiece.

The next morning it was gray and misty. We were staying at the Alamac Hotel, at 71st and Broadway, and when we woke up and looked out the window we didn't think there would be a game. It was a miserable day. Ordinarily we would have been out at the ball park by eleven thirty, but the day was so gloomy we just sat around the lobby waiting for word. Then Judge Landis called up and said, "Get your asses out there, boys, we're going to play." So we piled into taxicabs and headed up to the Stadium.

That number seven was a good ball game. In fact it was a great Series, any way you look at it, what with some good pitching and some very heavy hitting. But it was also a dramatic Series, for the simple reason of Alexander in that last game. I think it's one of the most dramatic things in all of baseball history, because it was Grover Cleveland Alexander who was involved. Anytime you have a really great athlete who's at the twilight of a long career come in and rise to the challenge, it's truly something to see and to remember.

After the sixth game, which Alec had pitched and won for us, we went into the clubhouse and Hornsby said to Alexander and Sherdel, "Alec, you're in the bull pen tomorrow and Sherry, you're in the bull pen."

Sherdel just nodded; it was fine with him. But Alec said, "All right, Rog. But I'll tell you, I'm not going to warm up down there. I've got just so many throws left in this arm. If you need me, I'll take my warm-up pitches on the mound."

And that's the way it was left. So when you hear those stories about how Alec didn't think he might be called on the next day and was out all night celebrating and how he was hung over when he came in, it's a lot of bunk. I saw him around the hotel the night before, for goodness sakes. I don't say he didn't have a drink, but he was around most of the night.

Haines started the seventh game for us and he pitched just fine. We got three runs in the fourth inning and I'll tell you, I should have got credit for a base hit on the ball that Koenig got his hands on. Why sure I remember it. You certainly do remember those hits that they took away from you. I can tell you just what happened. We were losing 1–0 to Ruth's home run. Then in the top of the fourth Jim Bottomley got a hit. I came up and hit one way over in the hole on the left side. Koenig went far to his right and fumbled the ball. They gave him an error on it but there was no way he could have thrown me out even if he had handled it cleanly. No way.

Then Chick Hafey lifted a little fly ball that fell into short left for a hit and the bases were filled. And then came a big break. Bob O'Farrell hit a fly ball to Meusel in left-center and Meusel dropped it. Just like that. Easiest fly ball you ever saw. What must have happened was he had set his mind on getting that ball and throwing home to try and catch Bottomley—Meusel had an outstanding arm. So he might have been thinking more about throwing it than catching it and maybe that's what brought about the error. But, gee, when that ball popped out of his hands the silence in that big ball park was really stunning. It was a hometown crowd, of course, and they couldn't believe what they had seen. Nobody could.

Then came the last of the seventh. The score was 3–2 now. With two out they loaded the bases against Haines and Tony Lazzeri was up. Haines was a knuckleball pitcher. He held that thing with his knuckles and he threw it hard and he threw it just about all the time. Well, his fingers had started to bleed from all the wear and tear, so he called a halt. Rog and the rest of us walked over to the mound.

"Can you throw it anymore?" Rog asked him.

"No," Jess said. "I can throw the fastball but not the knuckler."

"Well," Hornsby said, "we don't want any fastballs to this guy."

You see, we had been throwing Lazzeri nothing but breaking balls away and had been having pretty good luck with him.

So Rog said, "Okay, I'm going to bring in Pete," which is what we sometimes called Alexander.

So in came Alec, shuffling through the gloom from out in left field.

You ever see him? Lean, long, lanky guy. An old Nebraskan. Took his time at everything, except pitching. Then he worked like a machine. That arm going up and down, up and down. If you didn't swing at the first pitch it was strike one, you didn't swing at the second pitch it was strike two. If he walked two men in a game he was wild. His control was amazing, just amazing. He could thread a needle with that ball. When he told you he was going to pitch a hitter a certain way and wanted you to play accordingly, you did it and that's all there was to it.

He came in there cold, took eight warm-up pitches on the mound and he was ready.

He wanted to get ahead of Lazzeri. That was his idea. But it had to be on a bad ball. He was going to throw that first one fast to Lazzeri, high and tight, far enough on the inside so that even if Lazzeri hit it solid it would have to go foul, because in order to get good wood on it, Tony would have to be way out in front with the bat. If he didn't get good wood on it, then he would be hitting it on the handle and maybe breaking his bat.

What made him think Lazzeri would be swinging at a bad ball? Well, Alec was a little bit of the country boy psychologist out on that mound. I guess a lot of your great pitchers are. He knew it was Lazzeri's rookie year, and that here it was, seventh game of the World Series, two out and the bases loaded and the score 3–2. Lazzeri *had*

Grover Cleveland Alexander in 1926

Tony Lazzeri

to be anxious up there. This is not to take anything away from Lazzeri—he later became a great hitter—but at that moment he was a youngster up against a master. And don't think when Alec walked in it wasn't slower than ever—he wanted Lazzeri to stand up there as long as possible, thinking about the situation. And he just *knew* Tony's eyes would pop when he saw that fastball.

There are so many legends associated with that strikeout. For instance, they say Alec was drunk, or hung over, when he came in. And they say that Hornsby walked out to left field to meet him, to look in his eyes and make sure they were clear. And so on. All a lot of bunk. It's too bad they say these things. Now in the first place, if you stop to think about it, no man could have done what Alec did if he was drunk or even a little soggy. Not the way his mind was working and not the way he pitched. It's true that he was a drinker and that he had a problem with it. Everybody knows that. But he was not drunk when he walked into the ball game that day. No way. No way at all, for heaven's sake. And as far as Hornsby walking out to meet him, that's for the birds too. Rog met him at the mound, same as all the rest of us.

So after the conference on the mound we all went back to our positions and Alec got set to work. Sure enough, the first pitch to Lazzeri is the fastball in tight, not a strike. Well, Tony jumped at it and hit the hell out of it, a hard drive down the left field line. Now, for fifty years that ball has been traveling. It has been foul anywhere from an inch to twenty feet, depending on who you're listening to or what you're reading. But I was standing on third base and I'll tell you—it was foul all the way. All the way.

And then you should have seen Tony Lazzeri go after two breaking balls on the low outside corner of the plate. He couldn't have hit them with a ten-foot pole.

Then Alec shuffled off the mound toward the dugout. I ran by him and said something like, "Nice going, Alec." He turned his head toward me and had just the shadow of a smile on his lips. Then he took off his glove and flipped it onto the bench, put on his Cardinal sweater and sat down.

You know, a lot of people think that Lazzeri strikeout ended the game. You'd be surprised how many people I've spoken to through the years think it was the ninth inning. But hell, we still had two more innings to go.

Alec handled them like babies in the eighth, one, two, three, just like he knew he had to. In the bottom of the ninth they had their good hitters coming up—Combs, Koenig, Ruth, then Meusel and Gehrig.

Combs led off. He could run like a deer and I had to play in on the grass. He hit a doggone ball down to me and I got it in between hops and threw him out. Then Koenig came up and *he* hit one down to me off the end of the bat, spinning like crazy. I went to my right, picked it up and threw *him* out. You know, now and then during the winter I'd suddenly stop whatever I was doing and say to myself, "Boy, I wonder what the hell would have happened if I'd messed up one of those plays?" Those are the things you think about later.

So Ruth came up with two out and nobody on, just as Alec had wanted it. It would be nice to say that Alec struck him out to end it, and he nearly did. He nearly did. He took Babe to a full count and then lost him on a low outside pitch that wasn't off by more than an eyelash.

Ruth got to first and then, for some reason I've never been able to figure out, tried to steal second. Bob O'Farrell gunned the ball down to Hornsby, Rog slapped on the tag and that was it.

We all froze for a second, then rushed at Alec. We surrounded him, the whole team did, and pounded him around pretty good. He kept nodding his head and smiling and saying very softly, "Thanks, boys, thanks."

So many other things have come and gone now through the years. It's a long time ago, isn't it? More than fifty years. But whenever I think of Alec walking in from left field through the mist, it seems like yesterday. I can see him yet. . . .

Tom Seaver

GEORGE THOMAS SEAVER

Born: November 17, 1944, Fresno, California
Major League career: 1967–   New York Mets, Cincinnati Reds

One of the finest pitchers in the history of the National League, Tom Seaver's accomplishments are many and glittering. He holds the major league records for most consecutive seasons with 200 or more strikeouts (9), most consecutive strikeouts in a game (10), and is tied for most strikeouts in a game (19). He also holds the National League record for most strikeouts by a right-handed pitcher (289). Seaver has three times been voted the National League's Cy Young Award.

THE THING I was looking forward to most that winter was Opening Day, 1970. That was when we were going to get our World Series rings. It's got to be one of the greatest moments for a ball player. That ring is a lasting thing. When all the shouting has faded, when everybody has gone their separate ways, and the dust is beginning to collect on the scorebooks, you've still got that beautiful ring. It not only tells you that you were World Champions, but it also helps keep vivid all of those fine relationships you had with your teammates. It's the symbol of all of those people working together toward the single goal and achieving that goal.

I guess I first started becoming aware of the World Series in the early 1950's, when I was about eight or nine years old, growing up in Fresno, California. I remember it was a Dodger–Yankee Series and I was pulling for the Dodgers because they were the underdogs. Everybody was an underdog against the Yankees in those days, weren't they? When the games were on television I would get "sick"—a case of World Series fever—and my mother would let me stay home from

103

Tom Seaver

school. I wasn't fooling her, of course; she diagnosed my "illness" perfectly, but being a very understanding person she let me stay home. Also, she was quite a baseball fan in her own right and didn't want to watch the games by herself.

We would sit and watch every pitch of every game. But you know, the thing that really fascinated me was when the TV cameras went into the winning clubhouse when it was over. I saw the elation and the jubilation and I always thought that that was the ultimate—getting into the clubhouse and pouring champagne over each other's heads. Then when we did win it all, in 1969, and I was a part of it, I found out that the celebration was really secondary. It wasn't the ultimate moment at all. The ultimate moment came during the competition out there on the field. But you have to experience that to know it.

Another thing I didn't realize when I was a youngster home watching it on TV, was that there are hordes of people covering those games. When we won our division, against the Cardinals at Shea Stadium, it was probably the most joyous moment I had. The coverage was just the local press, our own guys. The clubhouse wasn't jam-packed afterwards. Then when we won the National League pennant, against the Braves at Shea, there were more people, more cameras. And when we won the World Series against Baltimore, again at Shea, the clubhouse was packed.

What I wanted to do after winning that World Series was get into the clubhouse and share the joy and the excitement and the satisfaction with the guys I had played with, like Buddy Harrelson and Jerry Grote and Cleon Jones and Tommie Agee and Jerry Koosman and all the others. I wanted more than anything else to enjoy that spontaneous sharing with my teammates while the victory was still warm and fresh and still tingling, while the emotional high was still climbing. But I never had that opportunity, because we had in effect been invaded. One group of reporters had one guy cornered here, another group had another guy cornered there, the TV people were grabbing us for interviews. It was absolute bedlam. We just couldn't get near one another, and that aspect of it was a great disappointment.

On the other hand, that experience did give new dimensions to my perceptions of what the World Series is, what it represents. It's like the Fourth of July, New Year's Eve, and your birthday all wrapped in one. The number of people that become involved in it is incredible. Once that last out is made everything becomes a madhouse.

I asked Buddy Harrelson once what he remembered most when he thought about that World Series. He said it was Cleon making the catch in left field for the final out and then going down on one knee like he was in prayer, holding like that for a split second and then making a beeline for the right field bull pen to get into the runway leading back to the clubhouse. You see, we'd had some experience with the enthusiasm of the Met fans. As I mentioned earlier, we had clinched the division title and won the league pennant both at Shea and each time the outpouring of fan enthusiasm got progressively worse. So Cleon knew he had to get out of there, before 57,000 people came storming out to offer congratulations.

Between the Dodgers, Giants and Yankees, New York had certainly seen plenty of World Series through the years. But in 1969 you would have thought it was the first one. The city just seemed to go wild. After we'd won it we were given a parade down Fifth Avenue—a victory celebration. You know, somebody said that celebrity parades are rated in enthusiasm by the amount of refuse that is accumulated. Well, we beat out the astronauts for first place by something like seventeen tons of paper, or some such outlandish figure. The Mets were unbeatable that year, even in parades.

You see, up until that time the Mets had no record of winning. That's what made the whole thing so stunning. The club had been in existence only a few years and its record was one of mediocrity. As an expansion team, the ball club had no real history or tradition, nothing for the fans to point to or build their hopes upon. Sometimes memories of better days can sustain you during hard times. But there was nothing to remember. The only thing the Mets were known for was losing. But in one season we changed that.

We were pegged as a 100–1 shot in spring training, and some people thought even that was being charitable. But that never bothered us. We didn't pay any attention to it. We knew we were a good ball club and we sensed what was going to happen a lot earlier than anybody else. They called us "The Miracle Mets." Miracle my eye. What happened was that a lot of good young players suddenly jelled and matured all at once: Harrelson, Grote, Agee, Koosman, Swoboda, Kranepool, Jones, and a lot of others. The chemistry on that ball club was a beautiful thing to feel and to see in action. Everybody had to contribute because we weren't that powerful, and everybody did contribute, from Al Weis and Rod Gaspar to Donn Clendenon and Ken Boswell and Art Shamsky and Wayne Garret, and all the others. I guess there have been some great ball clubs that have pretty much won it with their eight regulars and pitching staff; but the '69 Mets needed every man.

We got a certain momentum going that summer and it just never stopped. It kept building. I think we all really started to feel it when

Gil Hodges, left, working out with Jerry Koosman

we beat the Dodgers in a series early in the season—I remember Willie Davis made an error that gave us a ball game. If it's possible to put your finger on the one moment when we all began to feel it and believe it, that might have been it. I swear, it was like electricity going through the team. Everybody felt the same charge. We began getting stronger and stronger and feeling more and more confident. It went on from there, building.

There was no great mystery to it. We just kept winning, that's all. It was a classic pattern: good pitching, timely hitting, solid defense, hustle, self-confidence. People kept waiting for the bubble to burst, but it never did and we knew it wouldn't. I've got to give a lot of credit to Gil Hodges, our manager, and to Rube Walker, our pitching coach. They stayed very calm and cool about everything. They had been through a lot of pennant races with the Brooklyn Dodgers, remember, so they knew what it was all about. They knew what to look for, what to expect. Anytime we started to flutter a little bit they straightened us out.

The job they did handling the pitching staff was absolutely first-rate. Going into September our pitching was just as strong as it could be. We didn't have any tired arms. Why, coming down the stretch I won my last ten starts and Koosman won his last nine. We had a good staff. Along with Koosman and myself, there was Gary Gentry, Nolan Ryan, Don Cardwell, Jim McAndrew. And between Tug McGraw and Ron Taylor, a heck of a bull pen. We had some real hard throwers. I could zing it in there pretty good, and you know all about Nolan Ryan. Gentry could really fire, and Koosman had an incredible inside fastball to right-handed hitters. He made a lot of them jump away, only to have that ball come back into the strike zone. His ball just exploded.

How did I feel about starting in a World Series? Nervous. I've always been fascinated by baseball history, by all the myths and the legends, going all the way back to Christy Mathewson. That weighed on my mind, I'm sure. Being familiar with all of that history and suddenly looking up and being a part of it, the next actor walking out onto the stage, can make you nervous. What you do is going to be written down and recorded and become part of that history. There's no question that it weighed on my mind.

I didn't have a very auspicious beginning. The second pitch I threw was hit by Don Buford over the right-field fence for a home run. That's getting a new ball in play in a hurry, isn't it? They got three more runs in the fourth inning, we couldn't do much with Mike Cuellar and the final score was 4–1.

I think a lot of people wrote us off right then and there. It was as if they were saying, "Well, those guys were lucky for a hundred sixty-two games and were lucky against Atlanta in the championship series and now their luck has run out." Well, if they could have come into our clubhouse after that game they would have thought differently. The atmosphere in there was unbelievable, when you consider the fact that we had lost.

Remember now, Baltimore had a great team, no question about it. Solid hitting, good defense, first-class pitching. Statistically, they had

Frank Robinson

us outgunned at practically every position. Look at that team: Boog Powell, Frank Robinson, Brooks Robinson, Dave Johnson, Don Buford, Paul Blair, Mark Belanger, Andy Etchebarren, plus great pitchers like Cuellar, Jim Palmer, Dave McNally. That team won 109 games that year. They were going to win two more pennants. So they were over-whelming favorites. And naturally the odds jumped even higher after they won the first game.

But a funny thing happened after that game. I think Baltimore might have been just a little bit deceived by the ease with which they won it. They ran off the field like crazy, full of exultation. But the feel-ing we had when we got into our clubhouse was that they had just barely beat us. Never mind the score; a team knows if they've been badly beaten or outplayed. And we felt we hadn't been. We hadn't been more than a hit or two away from turning it around. The feeling wasn't that we had lost, but, *Hey, we nearly won that game.*

I think the man who realized it more than anyone else was Donn Clendenon. I can very distinctly remember Clendenon saying, "We're going to kick hell out of these guys." He started talking about it and the next thing you knew we were building more confidence out of having *lost* a game than if we had won it. We hadn't disgraced ourselves, as the odds-makers suggested we might. We realized we could win. It hit us like a ton of bricks. I tell you, that was the chemistry we had on the '69 Mets, these sudden surges of every-body thinking alike.

The next day we set out to prove it. Jerry Koosman pitched a power-ful game, a two-hitter. In fact they didn't get their first hit until the 7th inning. Jerry beat them 2–1.

Then Gary Gentry and Nolan Ryan teamed for a 5–0 shutout in the third game. That was the game Tommie Agee made one of his incredible catches, sliding on his belly to take a hit away from Paul Blair with the bases loaded. You know, a funny thing about a ball player's man-nerisms on the field. Tommie had a habit of hitting his glove with his hand when he knew he could catch a ball. Well, if you look at the films of those great catches, you'll see him doing that. It's really re-markable—nobody else thought he could get to that ball, but Tommie knew, because he punched his glove as he took off after it. And sure enough, he caught it.

I started the fourth game and had very good stuff. I hooked up against Cuellar again and had them shut out 1–0 to the top of the ninth. That one run was a Donn Clendenon shot over the left-field wall.

I got Paul Blair to fly out to start the inning. Then Frank Robinson came up. Now, I had been pitching away from him the whole game and had handled him pretty well. In fact, in both starts he hadn't had a hit off of me. Pitching him away, you see. But then in the ninth inning I came in inside and boy, he ripped one into left field. I mean, he crunched it. Why did I go inside to him? Well, I was trying to be smart. Trying to be a pitcher. I figured he would be looking for me outside. And maybe he was, but if so he sure adjusted in one hell of a hurry. You just can't mess around with those great hitters. That's hard-won knowledge and most of the time you apply it, but now and then you decide to get cute.

Then Boog Powell bounced a single over Kranepool's head and Robinson went to third. Brooks Robinson came up and hit a drive to right-center on which Swoboda made a spectacular diving one-handed grab. Frank Robinson scored after the catch to tie the game. It was a little disheartening, I suppose, to have gone into the ninth up 1–0 only to see them tie it up. But it could have been worse.

We won it in the bottom of the tenth with the help of a flukey play. Jerry Grote opened with a double. Al Weis got an intentional walk and J. C. Martin was sent up to hit for me. He laid down a bunt, Pete Richert picked it up and fired it to first base. The ball hit Martin on the wrist and rolled away and Rod Gaspar, who was running for Grote, came home with the winning run. It was a controversial play because the Orioles claimed Martin had run out of the baseline, and I think the films later showed that he had. But it was too late then and we won it, 2–1.

The next day Koosman pitched another beauty and beat them 5–3 to give us the championship. Koosie's such a cool character. I don't think I've ever seen him nervous. They had him down 3–0 early in the

Tom Seaver

game but it didn't seem to bother him. Nothing ever seemed to bother him. In that game the Baltimore pitcher, Dave McNally, came up in the second inning in a bunt situation, swung away and hit a home run. Then Frank Robinson came up later in the same inning and hit one out. Koosman never blinked an eye. He just stayed out there and kept firing away, waiting for us to come back.

In the sixth inning there was another one of those fluke occurrences. Cleon Jones was hit on the foot with a pitch, but the umpire at first said he hadn't been. Then Hodges came out and there was a big discussion and they found shoe polish on the ball. So they gave Cleon first base. Then Clendenon hit a home run. In the next inning Al Weis, who had hit only two home runs all year, hit one into the left-field stands to tie it up.

The winning runs came in the eighth, on a couple of doubles by Jones and Swoboda and then some loose play in the Baltimore infield. I can still see Swoboda's double going down the left-field line. It's strange how certain things stay with you. Of course that was the hit that drove in the winning run, so it's a reasonable memory to carry, isn't it?

A few minutes later, that pandemonium I told you about broke out, on the field and in our clubhouse.

My wife and I took off for the Virgin Islands right after the Series. Things had become so hectic, the phone just never stopped ringing. So we went down to St. Thomas for about ten days. Nobody knew where we were. It was beautiful. We had this lovely house overlooking the bay. Champagne breakfasts. Tropical sunsets. We just sat there and let it sink in: World Champions.

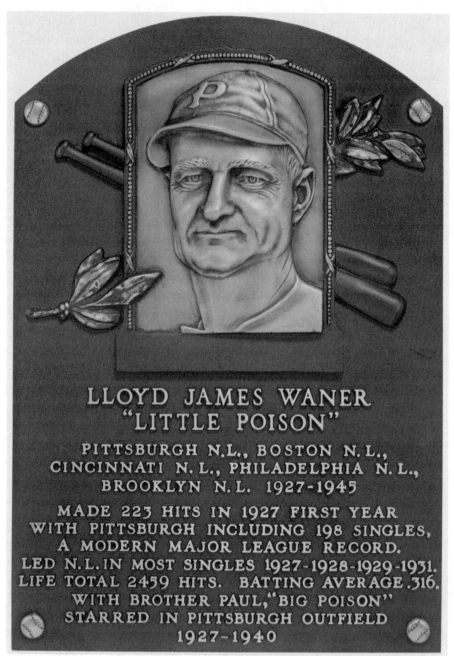

Lloyd Waner Hall of Fame plaque

Lloyd Waner

SOME PEOPLE find it unusual for two brothers to have gone up to the big leagues and had long careers and in fact ended up in the Hall of Fame together. Well, the way I look at it, Paul and me had an advantage over most kids. There was only two years and eleven months difference in our ages, so we never lacked for somebody to play with. We loved baseball and we played together all the time. Seems we were always swinging something, be it a broomstick or a plain old stick or whatever was handy. Our Dad made sure we had something to swing, and he'd make us a baseball out of old rags and twine.

We were always pitching to each other, be it one of those old rag-and-twine balls, or else corncobs. That's right, corncobs. We would break them in two and then soak them in water so they'd go farther when we hit them. You couldn't help but to develop quick wrists swinging at those things because they broke in every direction. It was almost impossible to throw one straight. Broomsticks and corncobs. That's the beauty of baseball—anybody can play it and it doesn't have to be done too fancy.

I was born on a farm in Harrah, Oklahoma. Same place as my big brother. We had a really nice farm. At first we had cotton, but then the boll weevil started taking the cotton, so my Dad switched to alfalfa hay and wheat and corn and all sorts of vegetables.

My Dad had been a professional ball player himself you know, in Oklahoma City, when they first had the Western League. This was back in 1898. To get to the games he would ride his horse to Oklahoma City, leave it in the livery stable and then join the team. His salary was fifty dollars a month. But that looked like big money in those days. They played only three games a week, plus holidays.

He was a pretty good player, Dad was. As a matter of fact, at one

Lloyd Waner in 1928

time Cap Anson made him an offer to join the White Sox, but he didn't want to leave the farm. I guess not too many people remember Cap Anson's name today, but he was one of the greatest ball players of the last century.

Dad liked to kid Paul and me. When we were in the major leagues the roster was set at twenty-one players, not twenty-five like they have today. Well, he'd tell us that was pretty soft, because in his day, in the Western League, a club would carry only ten players. He was a pitcher and when he wasn't pitching, he said, they generally would put him in the outfield. Of course they played just three games a week, so we'd kid him back and tell him *that* was pretty soft.

He encouraged us to play ball. He sure did. Every chance he had he took us out to play catch. Now Dad was a good pitcher and he took some pride in that, especially in the curve ball he could throw, and it was a darned good one, too, very fast breaking. So when we went out to play catch he tried to take it easy, because we were so small. Also, we didn't have a catcher's mitt. I mean we had one, but Paul was left-handed and the mitt was right-handed. It was all right for me because I threw righty. So when Paul was catching Dad he had to do it with the mitt on the wrong hand. When Dad wanted to throw one of his great curve balls he'd tell us it was coming. Finally one day Paul said to him, "Throw anything you want. Don't make any difference, curve or not." So Dad figured he'd teach us a lesson and started mixing those pitches up, curves and fastballs. But we surprised him by catching everything he threw, and Paul especially surprised him because Paul had that mitt on the wrong hand.

Finally Dad stopped and put his hands on his hips.

"You fellows are all right," he said. "I'll swear, I'm throwing my best curves and I can't even fool you. You fellows sure have quick little hands."

I was around eight years old at the time and Paul was eleven.

Then Dad liked to see a good footrace. Every month or so he would measure off a hundred yards by strides and mark it off. Then he'd turn us loose. For a long while Paul used to beat me by a step or so. That was when we were younger. But then, after a while I started beating him until it got to where I was a step or two faster at a hundred yards than he was. And Paul could fly. But it was more than just a footrace, because my Dad used to coach us. He taught us to run on our toes, which he said was the main thing. You can't run fast if you're running flat-footed.

Dad managed a local team for a while, and one day he put me into the game as a pinch-hitter. I never will forget it. I was just twelve years old at the time and here I was getting into a game with grown men. I was so small that the other team thought Dad had put me in to try and work out a base on balls. But I hit at the first pitch I saw and poked it over the third baseman's head down the left-field line. We were playing in a cow pasture and the ball rolled into some weeds and got lost. I started running, so excited I was shaking. When I got to third base they were still out in the weeds looking for the ball. I stood there and didn't know what to do. Gee, I thought, the ball is lost. So I ran out there to help them look for it, too excited to hear my Dad yelling at me to come on across the plate. Well, they finally found the ball and whoever picked it up took one look at me and tagged me out. Dad never let me forget that one.

So you had that combination of things. The constant playing, the desire, the love for the game, the encouragement and good coaching from our Dad; it all helped to develop what God-given abilities we had.

We just had a lot of fun growing up, Paul and me. There was a river nearby and we'd go down there and fish some, set trout lines. Sometimes we'd go hunt possum. It was a nice time and a nice place for growing up.

Yes, Paul and me were always good buddies. Not only brothers but best pals. But you know, sometimes he'd get me in trouble. He was always egging me on to fight somebody. This one occasion has always stayed in memory. We were walking home from school—it was two-and-a-half miles from our farm to the schoolhouse—with some of the neighborhood boys. A gang of us were walking down the road. Paul started some trouble between me and a bigger boy. Finally the boy put his schoolbooks down in the road, hitched up his trousers and began rubbing his hands together.

Lloyd and Paul, Paso Robles, California, spring of 1933. "Not only brothers but best pals."

I looked him over and then whispered to my brother, "Paul, he's a whole lot bigger."

He whispered back to me, "Just grab him by the legs and you got him."

So the fight started and I did what Paul said. I grabbed that boy by the legs and tumbled him off the road into a ditch where he landed right in a sandbur patch. Do you know what sandburs are? That's a weed that has burs growing on it and those burs are like needles. They can really hurt. Well, that boy came out of there covered with those things and just a-hollering and mad as blazes. He seemed twice the size now. I took one look at him and lit out for home fast as I could, with that boy coming after me, and Paul yelling from down the road, "Grab him by the legs! Grab him by the legs!"

Paul went into professional baseball two years before I did. He went out to San Francisco to play in the Pacific Coast League. He told the scout who had signed him about me and the fellow came by a year or so later and signed me to a contract. He said they would give me the same as they gave Paul his first year, which was four hundred dollars a month. I thought I was getting rich—that was big money back then, in 1925.

I was playing for a semipro team in Ada when I signed up. San Francisco promised to pay the team one thousand two hundred and fifty dollars and my Dad the same amount. Dad wanted to use the money to get me through college. I'd promised him I would go to college after the season. Well, San Francisco reneged on the agreement and wouldn't pay the money. Paul talked to Joe Devine who was a scout for Pittsburgh, and Devine said I should get my release and Pittsburgh would sign me. Paul advised me to do it and I did what he said. I got my release and the Pirates signed me. That suited me just fine because Paul was already with the Pirates and naturally I wanted to play with him. I was farmed out to Columbia, South Carolina, in the South Atlantic League, had a big year there and joined Paul in Pittsburgh the next season, 1927.

That was half the fun, I think, playing with old Paul. I sure would have missed him if I had gone with somebody else. He helped me out a whole lot, too. There were some pitchers in the league I was having a little trouble with and he told me what I was doing wrong against them. He got me to open my stance against left-handers so I wouldn't pull away from them. And he would tell me not to pay attention to the pitcher until the ball was delivered so as not to be thrown off by the motion. Paul was always helping me, telling me a lot of little old things that made me a better hitter. The main thing he used to tell me was to hit down at the ball instead of up. He said that would give me a level stroke and I'd hit a lot of line drives. That's the way he did it and he'd hit them through that infield so fast they couldn't see them.

Paul used to lay the bat right on his shoulder and keep it there until the last second, and then with those strong wrists he'd whip it around and make that ball zing. I did it the same way. I never will forget some of the managers around the league saying we couldn't hit the inside pitch because we wouldn't be able to get the bat around on it. But the inside pitch never bothered us; in fact we hit it better. In our first three years together at Pittsburgh, Paul hit .380, .370, .336, and I hit .355, .335, .353, and we averaged better than 220 hits a season apiece. So we were making pretty good contact.

They used to call us "Big Poison" and "Little Poison." A lot of people have thought we had those nicknames because we were "poison" to the opposing pitchers. But that isn't the way it came about. It started in 1927, in New York. We were playing the Giants in the Polo Grounds. There used to be this Italian fellow who always sat in the center-field bleachers. He had a voice on him you could hear all over the ball park. When he hollered out you heard him no matter where you were.

Well, Paul and I were hitting well against the Giants. This one day we came out of the clubhouse between games of a doubleheader and this fellow started hollering at us. What it sounded like was "Big and Little Poison," but what he was really saying was "Big and Little Person." He was a real nice fellow and we would wave at him and he finally became our biggest rooter in the Polo Grounds. We got him an autographed baseball one time. But whenever we came in there he would yell that and the newspapermen finally picked it up, except they thought he was saying "Poison" instead of "Person." It became a

Chuck Klein hitting one in the 1933 All-Star game. The catcher is Rick Ferrell.

newspaper nickname, because no ball players ever called us that. And the name has stuck, right down to this day.

I thought that Bill Terry and Paul were the two best left-handed hitters in the league. And the best right-handed hitter was Hornsby. Boy, was he a hitter! You just didn't know how to play him out there because he would slam that ball where it was pitched. Line drives. Gee whiz, what line drives. He just powdered it. The only way to play him in the outfield was to try and get a jump on the ball, judging by his swing and where the ball was pitched. Joe Medwick was another great right-handed hitter, and so was Chick Hafey.

Lefty O'Doul was another top-notch batter back then. He was strictly a pull hitter, sending practically everything to right field. You would have thought we would have been able to defend against him, but yet he led the league in batting a couple of times. He just powdered that ball down the line so hard nobody had a chance to move for it. Chuck Klein was another fellow who hit the ball to right field most of the time. He was more of a fly-ball hitter. He whacked a lot of home runs. Klein had an advantage when he broke in because his home park was that old Baker Bowl with the short, high fence out in

Chick Hafey in 1930

right field. You didn't have to hit the ball good to make contact with that fence, you only had to get it up in the air, which Klein was able to do. But he wasn't a left-field hitter. I've always considered the good hitter the man you can't play on the straightaway, who can snap that ball into any field, like Bill Terry and Paul and Hornsby used to do.

We had a fellow with us on the Pirates throughout the 1930's who sure was an outstanding hitter and a fine shortstop. Arky Vaughan. I don't know why he's not in the Hall of Fame today. He's got a record that's better than a lot of them who are. He could hit and he could field and he could run. I'll say he could run. We had a contest on in Pittsburgh one time, things like running to first base, bunting and running, and so on. Arky and I tied in going to first base in bunting and running. Three and two-tenths seconds. Don't think that Arky Vaughan couldn't scamper. For going from home plate to second base I don't think there was anybody who could match him.

My first year up to the majors was 1927 and darn if we didn't win the pennant. Boy, I thought to myself, this looks like a cinch. But I hung around for eighteen more years and never saw another one.

We played the Yankees in the World Series that year. Of course everybody knows that the 1927 Yankees are supposed to be the greatest team ever put together, what with Babe Ruth, Lou Gehrig, Earle Combs, Bob Meusel, Tony Lazzeri, and the rest of them. The famous story that has come out of the 1927 World Series concerns the first day, when we were supposed to have watched the Yankees taking batting practice. According to the story, which I have read and heard so many times, Paul and me and the rest of us were sitting there watching those big New Yorkers knock ball after ball out of sight and became so discouraged that we just about threw in the sponge right then and there. One story that I've read I don't know how many times has me turning to Paul and in a whispery voice saying, "Gee, they're big, aren't they?"

Joe Medwick

Arky Vaughan. "I don't know why he's not in the Hall of Fame."

That was the story. Well, I don't know how that got started. If you want to know the truth, I never even saw the Yankees work out that day. We had our workout first and I dressed and was leaving the ball park just as they were coming out on the field. I don't think Paul stayed out there either. We never spoke of it. I know some of our players stayed, but I never heard anybody talk about what they saw.

I don't know where the story came from. Somebody made it up out of thin air, that's all I can say. Every time I hear that story I tell people it's not so, but it just keeps on going. I don't think Paul ever saw anything on a ball field that could scare him anyway. He was such a great hitter in his own right that he never had to take a back seat to anybody.

This is not to say we weren't impressed by those Yankees during that Series. We sure were. They were just a fine ball club. And Ruth, well, that fellow always impressed you. I can remember when the Yankees let him go and he came over to the National League with Boston. This was in 1935. He was old, he was fat, he couldn't run, and he had lost a lot of his ability up at the plate. But he was still Babe Ruth. He came into Pittsburgh to play and after one of the games, I was leaving the ball park to go home and there's Babe signing autographs, surrounded by this big crowd. I'll swear that half the people who were to the game were waiting for him to sign. I stood there for a while watching and marveling at it. When I went home that crowd was still around him. The next day when I came to the park, somebody told me that Babe finally asked one of the policemen to get him a folding chair and Babe just sat there signing autographs.

"Till how long?" I asked.

"Till nearly ten o'clock at night," the fellow said. "He just sat and sat and sat till he'd made everybody happy."

But that's the way he was. He would never disappoint anybody if he could help it. You don't find them like that very often, I daresay.

It was in Pittsburgh that Babe had his last great day on the field. You could see he was near finished. He still had that beautiful swing, but he just wasn't hitting them anymore. But this one day he upped and amazed everybody. He hit three of them out in one game. The last one was hit farther than any ball I've ever seen. It went over the roof. I was standing in center field watching it go. You would have thought it had a little engine in it. It became a dot against the sky and then disappeared. My, did he hit it. But he could hardly get around the bases. His legs were shot, you see. We hit several balls out to Babe in right field in that game and he could hardly move after them. It was sad watching him out there. Matter of fact, he retired shortly after that game.

But in 1927 Babe was still in top form and he showed very well in that Series. It's true the Yankees beat us four straight, but they didn't run us off the field. There was only one lopsided game, where they beat us 8–1. Otherwise two of those games were settled by one run, and it seems to me that every game was close going into the late innings.

No, I wasn't nervous playing in the World Series. I'll tell you the only time I ever felt that way on a ball field—when I played my first major league game. After that I was never nervous again on a ball field. That's the truth.

I started off the Series in good fashion. First time up, Waite Hoyt hit me with a pitch. Paul doubled me around to third—he had a nice habit of doing that—and I scored on a fly ball. Later on in the game I doubled and came in on a base hit.

Ray Kremer pitched for us and he worked a good game. What beat him was errors. The Yankees got three runs in the third inning and I don't think a one of them was earned. They beat us by a run, 5–4. That was too bad; we should have won it.

In the second game I led off with a triple against George Pipgras. I remember that clearly. George threw me a good fastball and I just laid my bat on it and poked it down the left-field line. Then I scored on a fly ball. That was another close one until the eighth when the Yankees got three runs. I think that score was 6–2.

The third game was the only one where they beat us real bad. It was 8–1. But even so, it was close until the bottom of the seventh when they got six runs. That was one of the things about that Yankee team —they could explode right in your face at any time. Lee Meadows had been going along just beautifully for us for six innings, and then *wham!* Six runs. Babe Ruth hit a home run in that inning with a couple of men on. But do you know, for all their power, they only hit two home runs in the Series—both by Ruth. Do you know who hurt us in that Series? Mark Koenig, the shortstop. He hit .500. We just couldn't keep that fellow off the bases. And he was batting in front of Ruth and Gehrig. That's what did us in more than anything else, that fellow always being on base when those big guys came up. I'll tell you another interesting statistic about that Series somebody recently pointed out to me. In the four games the Yankees struck out twenty-five times to our seven. But all the same, no matter how many things you look at, it's still who scored the most runs, isn't it?

Something people tend to overlook with that Yankee team is their pitching. Everybody talks about Ruth and Gehrig, and well they might, but that was one fine gang of pitchers they had. We saw four of them in the Series—Waite Hoyt, George Pipgras, Herb Pennock,

Herb Pennock in 1921

Wilcy Moore. Pennock was rough. In the third game he retired the first twenty-two batters. He had a perfect game going until one out in the eighth. I remember it was Pie Traynor who broke it up. Pennock had fine stuff and A-1 control. Remember, our club had a .305 team batting average that season, but Pennock smoothed us out with very little trouble. He wasn't the type who threw the ball past you— he just made you hit it right at somebody.

The fourth game was a close one all the way and had a very unusual finish. In fact, I wonder if any World Series game ever ended the way this one did. It was played in Yankee Stadium. I led off with an infield hit and came around to score the first run. Later on Ruth hit a home run to put them ahead by two runs, but then we scored two in the top of the seventh to tie it up. It went on into the bottom of the ninth that way, 3–3.

That bottom of the ninth was a real oddball inning. Johnny Miljus was pitching for us. He was a relief pitcher and a real hard thrower. He could burn it in. He started off the inning by walking Earle Combs. Then Koenig beat out a bunt. First and second now, with nobody out. Then Miljus made it even worse by letting go a wild pitch, moving the runners up to second and third, with no outs. And all the Yankees have waiting in line for us are Ruth, Gehrig, Meusel and Lazzeri.

Naturally in a spot like that we put Ruth on. So now it's bases loaded and Gehrig up. But I told you, Miljus could really fire the ball, and that's just what he did. He leaned back and let it go. Struck out Gehrig. Then he struck out Bob Meusel. All of a sudden it's two out and the bases are still loaded. Then he got one strike across on Lazzeri. I was standing out in center field and I was beginning to think, "Maybe we'll get out of it yet."

Miljus wound up and he fired the next one, but it went into the dirt and got away from the catcher, Johnny Gooch, and rolled all the way back to the screen. Combs ran home and the game was over. The World Series was over. For a couple of seconds I didn't budge, just stood out there in center field. Couldn't believe it, I guess. It's no way to end a ball game, much less a World Series, on a doggone wild pitch.

That's how they scored it, a wild pitch. But Johnny Gooch said later that he should have caught it. Well, no matter. It was all gone and done with.

We were a little unhappy with the way things had gone. We thought we were going to give a better showing than we did because we were a good hitting team, with Pie Traynor, Glenn Wright, Joe Harris, George Grantham, Clyde Barnhart, Paul and myself. In the Series I hit .400 and Paul .333, which wasn't bad. We outhit Ruth and Gehrig.

Paul and I went into vaudeville that winter. That's right. We were a vaudeville act. We traveled on the Loew's Orpheum circuit. We played ten weeks, going from St. Louis to Baltimore to New York where we played Loew's State for two weeks, then on to Pittsburgh and San Francisco and Los Angeles. Ten weeks altogether. We'd come out on the stage in our uniforms and play catch and tell some jokes about Babe Ruth and the World Series. Paul would go on the stage first and start calling into the wings asking where I was. Finally I'd run out with a ball in my hand and say, "I was running after the ball that Babe Ruth hit." The audience thought that was a good one.

Then we'd play burn-out. That was throwing the ball back and forth at top speed, making it pop in our gloves. Paul would say something like, "Say, you're pretty good." And I would say back to him, "You ought to see my brother." The people got a big kick out of it.

Then we played some music. You see, when we were going to school Paul took some lessons on the saxophone and I tried the violin. I never could get the hang of that thing, but I could carry a tune. So after the jokes and the running around on stage, the orchestra would strike up and we'd get our instruments and play along with them. Once in a while we'd hit the same note as the orchestra, but it didn't make much difference one way or the other because they made sure to play good and loud to cover us.

It was pretty good fun. We got a lot of standing ovations and sometimes had to come out and take a second bow. And we made more money those ten weeks in vaudeville than we did playing baseball for six months.

We did all right. They wanted us to go on for ten more weeks. But that would have thrown us over into spring training and the Pittsburgh ball club wouldn't let us do it. Paul was disappointed; he loved getting out there on the stage. But as far as I was concerned it was just as well. It had been a long season and I figured it was time to get on back home.

Ted Kluszewski

THEODORE BERNARD KLUSZEWSKI

Born: September 10, 1924, Argo, Illinois
Major League career: 1947–1961, Cincinnati Reds, Pittsburgh Pirates, Chicago White Sox, Los Angeles Angels
Lifetime average: .298

One of the mightiest power hitters of his era, Ted Kluszewski reached career highs in home runs with 49 and 47 in 1954 and 1955 respectively. In 1954 he led the National League in runs batted in with 141 and a year later in hits with 192. Kluszewski set a major league record by leading National League first basemen in fielding for five consecutive years. He also holds the runs batted in record for a six-game World Series (10) in the 1959 Series, during which he hit three home runs and batted .391.

THAT'S RIGHT, for all those years I had the reputation as being the strongest man in baseball. It seemed that any time a sportswriter had nothing to write about on a rainy day he'd write a story about how strong I was. I'd read those things and say to myself, "Boy, this is going to get me in trouble someday." You know how human nature is. People sometimes think it's fun to take a poke at a guy who has that kind of reputation. I can remember reading when Joe Louis was heavyweight champion how now and then somebody would walk up to him and take a swing at him, just for the hell of it, because it was Joe Louis. But luckily I never had any problems along those lines. It seemed that everybody went out of their way to be nice. And now that it's all safely in the past, I can let you in on a secret: I wasn't much of a fighter anyway.

It's true that I used to cut off my uniform sleeves and some people thought I was doing that to show off my biceps and maybe intimidate

Ted Kluszewski

the pitcher. Well, it might have looked that way, but that wasn't the reason at all. When I first came up with the Reds in the late 1940's the uniforms at that particular time were wool flannel and they never seemed to make an armhole big enough for me. I kept telling the guy who outfitted us to shorten the sleeves because they bothered me. But he didn't, for some reason, and so I took a scissors and did it myself. But it was strictly as a matter of comfort. I guess those big arms hanging out over the plate did look kind of menacing, but that was never my intention. Believe me, I was just a big peaceful guy trying to get a few base hits and make a living.

You know, in spite of my size, when I came up I was a spray hitter. During my first few years my home run totals were very modest, until 1953, when all of a sudden I hit forty. No, I didn't start swinging for the fences. It was the pitchers who forced me into hitting home runs. They found out they couldn't pitch me outside because I'd go with the ball. So they started coming inside. Well, if you adjust correctly you have to pull the ball, and when you pull the ball you just naturally hit more home runs. That's what happened with me.

Another factor in there was the idea of self-preservation for the pitchers. You see, when they were pitching me outside I was hitting a lot of line drives through the box. I must have been getting about a dozen pitchers a year with line drives, and they began thinking about that. I guess they figured they'd rather run the risk of throwing a home run ball than getting shot off the mound. And it was just fine with me. I hated hitting anybody with a line drive. I tell you, it's a damn scary thing to see somebody crumple up out there.

Anyway, I was able to adapt to the situation and make it work to my advantage. You can get a lot of advice, good and bad, but what it comes down to is what you can do with the talent that's inside you. I saw Rogers Hornsby frustrate the hell out of himself when he was managing our ball club in the early 50's. Now here was a guy who was perhaps the greatest hitter that ever lived—certainly the greatest right-handed hitter—and I don't think he ever quite understood why other ball players couldn't do what had been so simple for him.

Rogers was of the old school—there was only one way to do things:

Rogers Hornsby: "...I don't think he ever quite understood why other ball players couldn't do what had been so simple for him."

his way. He would say, "This is the way I did it and I hit four hundred. So this is the way you ought to do it." How can you teach somebody with that approach? A manager has a right to expect good performances out of his players, but at the same time he's got to be realistic. Hornsby seemed to forget that not everybody had been born with his eyes, his coordination, his judgment. That's a very special breed of cat, that .400 hitter, any way you look at him.

If I hadn't gone into baseball I probably would have played professional football. In fact, the whole baseball thing occurred kind of by accident. I was in my sophomore year at the University of Indiana, on a football scholarship, and already getting feelers from some of the pro teams. I wasn't a bad player; I could run, had good hands, good size.

I was sitting around one day and somebody told me that if you made the baseball team you didn't have to go out for spring football practice. So I made a very dedicated effort to make the baseball team, and I was successful.

One day during practice I hit a couple of balls hard—I always had good power. When we were through for the day the groundskeeper walked up to me.

"Hit 'em pretty good today, eh, kid?" he said.

"I guess so," I said.

"Ever think of following a baseball career?" he asked.

I laughed it off. The truth was, I didn't grow up dreaming about being a baseball player. I had played very little baseball as a kid; the big game in my neighborhood was softball.

Now this was 1945, the war was still on, and the big league teams were having to take spring training in the north because of wartime travel restrictions. The Cincinnati Reds were using the facilities at Indiana. We used the field in the afternoon and when we were finished with our practice the groundskeeper had to get it in shape for the Reds the next day. So he was around all the time and finally he mentioned me to the Reds.

"There's this big fellow who can hit the ball hard," he told them.

Well, I'm sure they'd heard that song before, but no matter how skeptical you might be, you always come out to see the big fellow who can hit the ball hard. Some Cincinnati people came around to watch me, and while I didn't sign a contract then they did talk to me and express interest.

Later on a few other clubs approached me, among them the Yankees and the Tigers. At that particular time I was an outfielder and when you looked at the Yankees and Tigers of that era you realized that as an outfielder you didn't stand much chance. They were pretty well stocked. Of all the interested parties, Cincinnati seemed to me to offer the quickest opportunity of getting to the majors. This was in 1946, and two years later the Reds took me to spring training with them.

Frankly, I didn't have expectations of making the team at that time. I think my fielding was suspect. But they brought Bill Terry in and I worked with him an hour a day before everybody else reported. That helped considerably. Then the regular first baseman, Babe Young, got sick and I had a chance to showcase myself. I had a very decent spring and by the end of the season I was the regular first baseman.

I'm not much of an authority on my own career, so you'll have to fill me in on some things as we go along. No, I don't read the record books very often. Some guys know every statistic for every year they played, but I never paid that much attention. But, hey, listen, of course I know I hit forty-nine home runs in 1954. I had about five games left to get that fiftieth and I really wanted it. I think I might have got just a little overanxious about it. You hit forty-nine home runs without swinging for them, and then you go all-out to get just one more and you can't get it. Is there a moral in there somewhere? Maybe. I'll leave it to you to figure out. Also, some of the pitchers weren't too happy about the idea of throwing it to me and I didn't get too many good balls to hit; as a matter of fact, I got quite a few bases on balls those last few games. I've always regretted not popping that last one. Not too many people have hit fifty home runs in one year.

After about a dozen years in the National League, mostly with Cincinnati, I suddenly found myself going over to the American League. It happened toward the end of August, 1959. I was waived out of the league and the White Sox picked me up. And I'll be darned if I didn't walk right into a World Series, for the first and only time in my playing career.

I'd never been on a team quite like that White Sox club. Al Lopez was the manager and he really had them going. It was a light-hitting club, with plenty of speed and hustle—guys like Nellie Fox, Luis Aparicio, Jim Landis, Billy Goodman—and a hell of a pitching staff. They had Early Wynn, Billy Pierce, Bob Shaw, Dick Donovan, Turk Lown, Gerry Staley.

They were altogether different from most of the teams I had played on in Cincinnati. In '56, for instance, we hit 221 home runs and tied a record, but finished third. Not enough pitching. Just a row of howitzers in the lineup—Wally Post, Gus Bell, Frank Robinson, Ed Bailey, myself. It was a lot of fun trotting around the bases all season, but we sure could have done with a little more pitching.

But that was a nice little dividend, that '59 World Series, coming as it did late in my career. Another nice thing about it was that it was in Chicago. I had grown up in Argo, a Chicago suburb, so it was like a homecoming for me. But, boy, what a ticket problem I had! They give

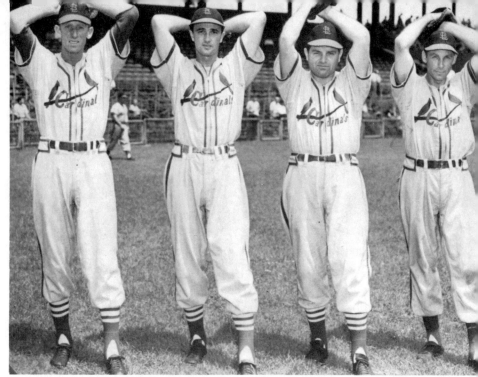

Four Cardinal left-handers: Left to right, Al Brazle, Howie Pollett, Max Lanier, and Harry Brecheen, in 1946. "I'll tell you who gave me more trouble than any other pitcher—Howie Pollett."

you plenty, but when you're playing in your hometown you can't get enough. I had so many friends out there, not to mention brothers, sisters, aunts, uncles, cousins. I tried to squeeze them all in for one game apiece; but I'll tell you, even if I had done it by innings I still don't think I could have got them all in.

No question about it, that World Series was the high point of my career. Just being there was enough, but then to cap it off I had a good Series. I'll never forget that first game in Chicago. It was the single most memorable day I ever had in baseball. In the first inning I came up against Roger Craig and singled to score a run. In the third inning I came up against Craig again, with a man on, and hit a home run. In the fourth inning I hit another home run with a man on. What a day! And just to make it perfect, Early Wynn and Gerry Staley combined to pitch a shutout, 11–0.

After that the Dodgers started to turn it around. I kept hitting all right, but the Dodgers were winning the ball games. They had some tough pitchers—Johnny Podres, Don Drysdale, Sandy Koufax, and Larry Sherry, who kept coming out of the bull pen to stop us.

They beat us in six games. That put a damper on it for me, because otherwise I had a great Series. I batted .391, hit three home runs, and drove in ten runs, which set a record for a six-game Series.

That's right, Koufax was in that Series. He was just coming into his own as a great pitcher. One of the best left-handers I ever saw. Spahn was another good one. But I'll tell you who gave me more trouble than any other pitcher—Howie Pollett. He was rough on me. I swear he could read my mind.

Yeah, I saw plenty of great ones while I was playing. Musial, Jackie Robinson, Mays, Aaron, Clemente. Mays was about as good as there was. I had a nice rapport with Willie. Sometimes when I was holding him on he'd put sand in my pocket. What with sweating and all, when I reached in there in the middle of the game to get some gum I'd come up with a handful of mud. I knew Willie had done it, and when

Henry Aaron, with Jacksonville, 1953

he came down there next time I'd step on his foot. But he was a great one. I don't think you can do it all any better than Willie did. And he was exciting out there. When he was on the field you just had to look at him. They call that charisma, I guess. I'm not sure I know just what the hell charisma is, but I get the feeling it's Willie Mays.

But there was another guy. *Everybody* watched him—the fans *and* the ball players. Everybody came to attention when Ted Williams stepped into the batter's box. He didn't have the Mays kind of flair, but he could hit so well. Finest hitter I've ever seen. He made contact with the ball so beautifully. He had the ability, the dedication, the style, and those high standards from which he never deviated. He just wouldn't swing at anything but a strike. I've swung at bouncing balls and pitches over my head; but I had to—I had to get that bat started. Williams didn't. He had the great eyes and he was quick. Every time he moved that bat it was a full swing; you never saw him make a false start.

It's a great game, a hell of a lot of fun, but boy, you never know. First day out in spring training in 1956 I reached for a ground ball and felt something go in my back. It was almost a year and a half before the problem was diagnosed correctly. I played a full season in 1956 but the pain kept recurring, coming and going. I'd be able to swing the bat great one day, then not be able to move the next. They eventually found out it was a slipped disc.

There was some talk about an operation, but I was dubious about going ahead with it. I checked with a specialist, just to be sure. He told me that the operation would be a complete success, but that I would lose a certain amount of mobility; not a lot, but enough to make the difference between being a ball player and just another guy walking down the street. The doctor told me, "If you can live with it, live with it." So I lived with it. I was never able to hit or move around as well as I had been, but I kept playing. But the peak years were gone.

No, I don't think an athlete finds it difficult to adjust psychologically to a limited career. He knows the meaning of the word "career" as it applies to him. It means being in the twilight at an age when other men are approaching their professional prime. We all know that after thirty there's going to be a decline somewhere along the way. If you're not prepared to accept that you're foolish to be in the game.

All the same, it isn't a pleasant thing to have to face. There's always the temptation to try that one more year, to see if you can wind up the clock again. But you find out soon enough that it's a game where youth dominates. You remember when you came up yourself, full of springtime, and pushed somebody else aside. So you have to be philosophical about it. You'd better be.

If you're lucky you can take some memories with you. For me the nicest will always be the first game of the 1959 World Series, in the sunshine in Chicago.

Ed Lopat in 1947

Ed Lopat

EDMUND WALTER LOPAT

Born: June 21, 1918, New York, New York
Major League career: 1944–1955, Chicago White Sox, New York Yankees, Baltimore Orioles
Lifetime record: 166 wins, 112 losses

Always a winning pitcher, Ed Lopat was known for his craft and control on the mound. One of Casey Stengel's solid triumvirate of Raschi, Reynolds and Lopat, "Steady Eddie" helped the Yankees to five consecutive pennants and world championships from 1949 through 1953, during which time he won 80 games and lost just 36. In 1953 he led American League pitchers in both winning percentage (.800) and earned run average (2.42). Lopat's World Series record is also an impressive one—4 wins and 1 loss.

No, I NEVER minded being called "The Junk Man." Never minded it at all. Actually the whole thing was contrived by a friend of mine named Ben Epstein. He was a newspaperman in Little Rock when I was playing there in the early 1940's. We were good friends and we remained good friends on through the years. When I was traded to the Yankees in 1948 Ben was working for one of the New York papers. He wrote an article about me for a sports magazine that year that he entitled "He's Got Plenty of Nothing." That was a reference to my style of pitching, which consisted of breaking stuff, changes of speed, control, and a hell of a lot of thinking. The season progressed and I kept winning. One day Ben came up to me and said, "Do you mind if I give you a nickname?"

"What kind of a nickname?" I asked.

"One that you'll have for as long as you're in the big leagues and that will be one of a kind."

141

"What is it?"

" 'The Junk Man,' " he said. "Do you mind?"

"Ben," I said, "I don't care what they call me as long as I can get those batters out and keep collecting my paycheck."

So that's how it got started. He began referring to me as "The Junk Man" in the newspapers and in magazine articles and it didn't take long for the name to catch on. The reason for the name, as I said, was because I wasn't an overpowering pitcher. I used to change speeds, move the ball in and out, throw everything with the same motion. Of course a lot of people who weren't too knowledgeable about baseball misconstrued the meaning of the nickname. They used to ask me how I could get the hitters out by throwing that garbage up there. They thought all I did was stand on the mound and throw slow pitches up to the batters. Well, I did throw a fair amount of slow pitches, but those things are effective only if you've set them up with harder stuff.

Now and then some American League hitters got the same idea— that I was easy to hit. Especially some of the new guys in the league, who had been reading about the "Junk Man." I could spot them right away, by the way they stood up there. They figured they'd be seeing one humpty-dumpty pitch after another. Well, I just threw the ball right past those guys. They caught on in a hurry. You see, I had the fastball and hard curve as well as the slider and screwball, and I changed speeds off of all of them. One thing the hitters always under-estimated was my fastball. That was my best "out" pitch when I had two strikes on a guy. They just never seemed to be looking for it. They were always looking for the "junk." Ben Epstein helped me with that nickname, no doubt about it.

I'll never forget one hot afternoon in Cleveland. We had a night game scheduled and I was starting. I generally had pretty good success against Cleveland. Anyway, the hotel wasn't air-conditioned and it was just miserable in there. I told Johnny Sain, "I'd just as soon go out to the ball park and sweat as sit here and do it." So we walked over to the ball park, which wasn't far from the hotel. When we got there we could hear the sound of baseballs being hit, which was puzzling since it was only four o'clock in the afternoon.

"What the hell's going on?" I asked Sain.

"Let's have a look," he said.

We went inside and walked up the ramp and from a discreet vantage point looked out on the field. The whole Cleveland club was there, rotating in and out of the batting cage. On the mound throwing to them was a left-hander, Sam Zoldak, whose style of pitching was similar to mine. He was throwing them big slow curves and they were standing flat-footed up there and hitting the ball to opposite fields. Getting geared for me, you see.

We watched for about twenty minutes and then slipped down to the clubhouse. Just before game time I told Berra about it.

"Listen," I said, "the first time around the horn we're not throwing anything slow. Fastballs and sliders, right in on them."

And that's what I did. I must have broken four or five bats. You could see how bewildered those hitters were. Each guy was coming up there looking for the slow stuff and here I'm beating a tattoo on their fists with fastballs and sliders.

I did that for about four innings until I could see them gradually going back to their old way of hitting. So I went back to my old way of pitching. I beat them easily that night.

The next day, when Cleveland was taking batting practice before the game, I went over to the cage. Al Lopez, the manager, was standing there with Tony Cuccinello, one of his coaches. I'd played with Tony on the White Sox and we were pretty good friends.

"Hey, you guys," I said. "Next time you want to hold a secret batting practice you ought to do it at ten o'clock in the morning when I can't watch it, because I don't get up that early."

"What are you talking about?" Tony asked.

"I saw that stuff you guys had going yesterday, with Zoldak out there throwing big slow curves."

Tony looked at me with a big grin and said, "You dirty so-and-so."

So you have to take advantage of every little thing, unless you have all the ability in the world, like a Ted Williams or a Bob Feller or a Joe DiMaggio.

Joe DiMaggio. Best player I ever saw. I say this with all due respect for Ted Williams. Williams was the better hitter, but for overall ability

Joe DiMaggio in 1937

Joe is tops. I had the opportunity to watch Joe from both sides of the fence because I played against him for a few years when I was with the White Sox and then played as his teammate on the Yankees.

What made me realize just how great DiMaggio was was something that happened during a game I was pitching in New York against Cleveland in 1948, my first year with the Yankees. This was around the middle of June. We were winning by either 2–1 or 3–2. I had two men on and two out and Lou Boudreau was up. In spots like that I would sometimes turn my back on the hitter and do a little thinking about how to start him off. I noticed Joe out there, playing straight-away in center. Then I turned around, got my sign and threw the first pitch. It was a ball. I was sort of perturbed with myself. When I got the ball back I turned around again, mumbling to myself, and there's Joe out in dead center, hands on knees, looking in. The next pitch was ball two. Now I was really upset with myself and didn't turn around.

I threw the next pitch and Boudreau stepped in and creamed it. He sent a line drive over Rizzuto's head. One of those vicious long line drives. The moment that ball left the bat I knew it was ticketed. Right into the left-center slot. A sure triple and two runs. When I turned around Joe was standing there, catching the ball without ever having moved. I was shocked, frankly.

When we got into the dugout after the inning I sat down next to him.

"Joe," I said, "I noticed you were in dead center on the first couple

"... for overall ability Joe is tops." Joe DiMaggio sliding safely into third. The third baseman is Eddie Yost, the umpire is Ed Hurley (all the way from home plate to cover the play), and the year is 1948.

of pitches. But then he hits the ball flush into the gap and you're standing right there."

"Well," he said, "I've seen you pitch enough times now to know how you work. I knew that as long as you stayed ahead of him or were even you wouldn't let him pull the ball. But when you went behind two balls and no strikes I knew you had to get the next one over and that he knew it too and would probably pull it."

Do you know how far over he moved before I threw that pitch? About eighty feet. That's when I said to myself, "No wonder this guy's a great player." And that's why you didn't see Joe make too many sensational catches. He knew the pitcher, the batter, the situation, and he played accordingly. He wasn't just a machine out there—he was a *thinking* machine.

That man's day-in-and-day-out determination on a ball field was something to see. If he went for the collar and we lost the ball game he would feel he let the team down.

When I was with the White Sox I was fairly successful pitching to Joe. Sometimes pitching and hitting is a battle of wits. You know what you're going to throw and the batter doesn't. Most of them hit after a certain pattern, especially the intelligent ones, like Williams and DiMaggio. If you got them out with a curve ball the first time, they went up to the plate the next time looking for it. They would take anything else you threw up there, until two strikes. Going under those assumptions, I used to try to pitch to those guys.

I can give you a good example with DiMaggio. One day in Chicago I got him out three times with screwballs. Three ground balls to short. He was fit to be tied. The next time I faced him was in New York and I knew he's got to be laying for that pitch. He was too experienced a hitter not to be. He came up in the first inning with a man on first and two out. I told myself I'd test him out with a fastball. The kind of pitch you ordinarily would never put in the strike zone to him. But I was convinced he was laying for the screwball. I threw it right down the pike and he never even flinched. That showed me right then and there that he's not looking for that pitch. Buddy boy, I said, you're getting another one. I threw the next one right down the middle and I swear the veins jumped up in his neck. That's how mad he was. He'd taken two fastballs right down the middle. Then I threw him the scroogie, just a little bad, and he hit it down to short.

But I still had to prove my point absolutely. In the seventh inning we had them beat 7–1 and Joe is leading off. I wanted to find out if he was still laying for the screwball. I gave it to him on the first pitch and he hit that thing nine miles into the left-field seats. That convinced me to keep the same pattern of pitching to him until he forced me to change it. With those kinds of hitters you've got to remember how you got them out and what the pitches were.

There are some hitters who just walk up there and swing. With these guys you try to pitch to their weakness the best way you can. But with a Williams or a DiMaggio, who were great hitters and intelligent at the plate at the same time, it becomes a battle of wits. But if you can throw four different pitches and the guy is up there looking for one of them, the odds are with you.

Later on, as I got older and more experienced, I learned that a hitter's reflexes could show me what he was looking for. That made it a lot easier for me. For instance, if you throw him a curve outside of the strike zone and he starts to swing and stops and takes it, you know he's waiting for the curve. He was so intent on watching for that curve, you see, his concentration was so intense, that even though the ball might have been a yard outside the strike zone, the moment his eye picked it up his anxiety was so great that he made the move to go after it. With some hitters all I needed to see was just the slightest flinch to tell me what I wanted to know. Then you think to yourself: If that ball was in the strike zone, did he have it timed perfectly, was he behind it, was he ahead of it? That governs your next pitch.

Now, these aren't guess hitters I'm talking about. These are guys who go up there looking for a certain pitch and who keep looking, up to two strikes. If they're looking for a curve and you throw one over the plate, they're going to knock the daylights out of it, no matter how good a curve it is. Because they're set for it. So the object of pitching to a "waiter" is not to give him the ball he's waiting for.

What you need is good stuff, control, know-how, and self-confidence. It doesn't hurt, either, to be a little of the psychologist out there.

Stengel was a great psychologist. One day we were playing a double-header in Detroit. We had given away the first game with some sloppy play. Errors, mistakes, the works. Then in the second game we tore them apart. By the sixth inning we had them by something like 16–2. But what do you think Stengel is doing? He's raising hell with every-body. He's like a raving lunatic. We're all sitting back wondering what in the world is wrong with him. Here we are running away with the game and he's tearing into everybody. Later on we found out why. We used to travel by train in those days. Well, after he'd had a few drinks, Casey would sit down with you and answer all your questions. A few of us got together with him on the train that night after we'd left Detroit.

"Case," somebody said, "what was the idea of raising so much hell in the second game?"

He winked, gave one of his wrinkled old grins and said, "You noticed that, did you?"

"How the hell could we not notice?" somebody said.

"Well," he said, "I've found out in past years that when a ball player is playing badly he knows it. He knows what he's done. I'm talking about good players, which we have on this club. Well, *that* is no time to hop on them because they're liable to turn around and punch you in the mouth. But when they're winning they'll take a lot more from you than they otherwise would. And not only that, but whatever you tell them then they'll absorb a lot better than they will when they're mad. Because when they're mad they won't listen."

That was a technique he used all the time. When he was sore about something and wanted to get it across he would always wait for the opportune time—and for him that was when things were going good and everybody was relaxed.

One thing I'll say about him—he never individualized in his criti-cism. When he held a meeting to get some things straightened out, he would talk in generalities; but the guys he was talking about always knew who he meant. That made his criticism—and he could be rough at times—more tolerable and, in my opinion, more effective.

Some guys didn't go along with Casey's approach to things. But he won a lot of pennants with the Yankees.

I got to the Yankees in a roundabout way. I was signed by the Dodgers first. That's right. The Brooklyn Dodgers. I went to a mass tryout at Ebbets Field one day. About a thousand kids showed up. It was quite a sight, all these kids running around out there in their different uniforms. Twelve of us were signed. This was in the fall of 1936. I was a first baseman then. A left-handed-hitting first baseman. In those years the Yankees had Lou Gehrig at first base, the Giants had Bill Terry, and I figured the Dodgers would have Ed Lopat. But it didn't work out quite that way. I switched over to pitching almost as soon as I got into pro ball.

The Dodgers sent me out to the minor leagues and then didn't exercise their rights of recall, so I became property of the minor league team. In those days a lot of those farm clubs were independently owned. I kept getting sold around the minor leagues. My record reads like a geography lesson: Jeanerette, Louisiana; Kilgore, Texas; Shreveport, Louisiana; Salina, Kansas; Longview, Texas; Greensburg, Pennsylvania; Oklahoma City. Oklahoma City sold me to Little Rock and from there I went up to the White Sox in 1944.

So I'd grown up in a city that had three big league teams, and when I finally come to the majors it's with the Chicago White Sox. Sure I wanted to be a ball player. That's all I lived for. When I was a kid I worked for a while as an usher at Radio City Music Hall. Some of the other kids talked about becoming actors or singers or this or that, but my dream was always baseball.

I was a Yankee rooter, but I seldom had a chance to go to a game. Those were Depression days and there was never enough loose change around for those kind of luxuries. The first big league game I ever saw was in 1933. The Yankees against the Washington Senators. Washington had a good ball club. I can still remember some of those guys—Joe Cronin, Buddy Myer, Heinie Manush, Goose Goslin. They won the pennant that year and played the Giants in the World Series.

Carl Hubbell, left, and Lou Gehrig in 1936

Jojo Moore in 1933

I would say the 1933 Series between the Giants and the Senators is the earliest one I can recall with good memory. The Giants had an outstanding team in those days, with Bill Terry, Mel Ott, Carl Hubbell, Jojo Moore, Hal Schumacher. They won the Series that year.

The following year it was the Cardinals and the Tigers. I was going to DeWitt Clinton High School at the time and I can remember cutting a class to listen to one of the games over the radio. You've got to do that at one time or another, I suppose, just to prove you're a good red-blooded American boy.

Another problem was I used to pass Yankee Stadium every day on the elevated train on the way to school. Now that was really putting temptation in front of a kid. Every now and then I *wouldn't* pass Yankee Stadium on the train and a group of us would get off and go to the ball game, cutting school.

Every school day for two solid years I rode that elevated train, winter and summer. From the train window I could see the grandstands and the green grass in the outfield, and sometimes I'd catch a glimpse of a game, seeing those little figures scattered out there. In the winter, when the field was covered with snow, I think I still saw them. I never got tired of looking at that ball park. So the dream stayed fresh, right in front of my eyes all the time. Seeing that ball park every day kept the dream *real*, if you know what I mean.

When it actually happened, when I got to the big leagues with the White Sox in 1944, I'll never forget coming out of the dugout in Yankee Stadium for the first time and looking around. I've got to admit it was quite a thrill. A lot of history had been made there, starting with Ruth and Gehrig. Since I'd grown up in New York and had always been a Yankee fan I was familiar with that history. When I was standing in the outfield during batting practice that first day I turned around and took a look out to where the elevated train ran beyond the bleachers, and I said to myself, "Well, they're watching *me* now."

After four years with the White Sox I was traded to the Yankees. That was the greatest thing that ever happened to me in baseball. It was a fantastic opportunity. My first year with the Yankees was 1948 and it was one of the few years that I was there that we didn't win the pennant. We were nosed out on the next to the last day of the season. It had been a three-way race and the Indians beat out the Red Sox in a play-off. Well, after four years in the second division with the White Sox, coming that close to first place really gave me an appetite for it.

Finally in '49 I was on my first pennant winner—just barely. We went into the last day of the season tied with the Red Sox, and playing the Red Sox. It's rare when the pennant race comes down to the last game of the season and even more unusual when you're playing your principal opponent in that game. Vic Raschi pitched all the way for us and beat them, 5–3. We got four of our runs in the last of the eighth and they got their runs in the top of the ninth. In other words, that game was 1–0 going into the bottom of the eighth.

It was one of the longest afternoons of my life, sitting on the bench and watching those innings go by. Believe me, the toughest part of a game like that is not being involved. If you're playing at least you get a chance to work off some of the tensions. But that bench starts to feel like pins and needles after a while. When we finally got the last out in the top of the ninth—Birdie Tebbets popped out to Tommy Henrich at first base—I thought the top of my head would come off.

Over in the National League, the Dodgers won the pennant the same way, on the last day of the season. So both teams went into the Series pretty keyed up. And of course the Dodgers and Yankees being natural rivals in those years, the Series was even more interesting.

I started the fourth game of the Series, in Ebbets Field. Some of the Dodger newspapermen didn't think I was going to have much luck, because that ball park was supposed to be a graveyard for left-handers, particularly with the right-handed hitting lineup the Dodgers had, guys like Pee Wee Reese, Gil Hodges, Roy Campanella, Jackie Robinson, Carl Furillo. As a rule, most left-handers used to sit it out in Ebbets Field. But it didn't bother me any. I didn't change my style of pitching. I went at it the same as always, changing speeds, throwing the screwball, pitching to spots.

Sure I was nervous starting that game. I never perspired much, and never through my top shirt. But I remember Bobby Brown coming

Carl Furillo in 1947

over from third base in the middle of the game and saying, "I've never seen you like this. You're soaking wet." "Nervous, that's all," I said. Nothing wrong with that. I've known guys who wouldn't ever admit they were nervous. But I felt better for saying it. Made me feel more relaxed. I felt the same way when I pitched my first game in the majors. You just can't escape it. What the hell, you're human. You remember what it was like to be a fan, how you sat around the radio hanging on every pitch. Well, all of a sudden you're the guy making those pitches and in back of your mind you know there's millions of people listening. A World Series has a special tension, and I'm not kidding. And unless you've been out there in the middle of it you can't really understand what I'm talking about. And of course a Yankee–Dodger Series had a little extra going for it.

Well, nervous or not, Ebbets Field or not, I pitched a pretty good game. I had them beat 6–0 going into the bottom of the sixth. Then they got a run and had a man on first and two out. Gil Hodges hit a ground ball right back toward me and to this day I don't know why I didn't pick it up. All I had to do was take a step and reach out for it and throw him out at first. But I just stood there and watched it. How do you explain those things? He got a base hit. Then they followed with three more hits just like that one—clunkers, humpbacked liners, a ground ball. They scored four runs and had the bases loaded. Stengel brought in Allie Reynolds and Allie was just sensational. He set down everybody he faced—ten men in a row.

I would have liked to have gone nine innings, but we won the game and that was all that mattered. Bobby Brown got the big hit for me, a triple off the right-field wall with the bases loaded. You see, everybody talked about the Dodgers' right-handed power being so threatening in Ebbets Field. Which it was. But what a lot of people forgot was that there was a very friendly wall out in right field and that we had some left-handed hitters who could really pepper it—fellows like Gene Woodling, Tommy Henrich, Yogi Berra, Bobby Brown. And that's just what they did. It seems to me we got quite a few extra base hits off of that wall. I even got one myself. I hit a double that knocked Don Newcombe out of the box in the fourth inning. If somebody had told me when the Dodgers signed me in 1936 that I wouldn't get my first hit in Ebbets Field until 1949 I might have got a little discouraged. But there it was.

The Dodgers had a good ball club, but going into the Series we were very confident. Confident, not cocky. Those Yankee ball clubs, for all their success, were never cocky. It just wasn't part of the Yankee makeup. But confident, you bet. And in a very quiet way. You always felt it in the clubhouse before a game. You don't realize how lethal it can be unless you've been on other ball clubs where that attitude didn't exist.

So we felt we would be able to beat them, and we did, in five games. What shocked them more than anything else, I think, was our beating them the last three games in their own ball park.

We won again the next year and this time we played the Phillies. We took four in a row from them. But it wasn't as easy as it looked. The games were all close. Low-scoring jobs. I pitched the third one, in Yankee Stadium. I went eight innings and left with the game tied. Tom Ferrick came in to work the ninth and he got the win when we scored a run.

That was Whitey Ford's first year, 1950. He joined the team in the middle of the year and did a magnificent job. They brought him along perfectly. As I recall, they started him against the second division clubs for a while and he pitched real well. I think he won his first eight games in a row. And then his true test came late in the season, against Detroit, the club we were battling neck-and-neck with at the time. We were caught short for a pitcher to open that series. So Stengel and Jim Turner, our pitching coach, said, "Well, we might as well see what the young fellow is made of," and they started him against Dizzy Trout. Whitey battled him 1–1 into the top of the ninth. Then we scored eight runs and Whitey won it easily. As far as we were concerned, that was his true test. He'd proved he could pitch under pressure.

That made his record 9–0. He lost only one game that year. It was a game where he relieved me in Philadelphia—the Athletics were still there then. I had them beat 2–0 in the bottom of the eighth and Gus

Zernial tied it up with a home run. They brought Ford in in the next inning. The Athletics loaded the bases against him and a fellow named Sam Chapman came up. Remember him? Pretty good hitter. Whitey threw him six curves in a row and on the sixth one Chapman got a base hit. That was the end of the game. Later in the clubhouse Whitey felt kind of bad, but we were kidding him about it.

"I'll bet you learned one thing," I told him. "You'll never throw six curves in a row to anybody again. Especially a good hitter."

That was one thing you could count on with Whitey—he'd never make the same mistake twice. For a young fellow he was fantastic.

So that was two years in a row I'd pitched in a Series. I was starting to feel like a World Series veteran. Also, I appreciated how lucky I was. I knew there had been a lot of great ball players like Luke

Whitey Ford

Mickey Mantle

Appling and Ted Lyons and others who had spent long careers in the big leagues and never played in a Series, and here I was, all of a sudden getting into two in a row. Gee, I thought, one more would be real nice.

And then it was three in a row, in 1951. I had a good year, winning twenty-one. That was the year the Dodgers and Giants went into a play-off, when Bobby Thomson hit his big home run. Where was I when Thomson hit it? Right there in the Polo Grounds with most of my teammates. We were all rooting for the Giants, because if they won it meant more money—the Polo Grounds accommodated about 20,000 more people than Ebbets Field. So when Thomson hit that home run we jumped up and started yelling like crazy.

The Series opened in Yankee Stadium that year and they beat us the first game. I started the second one, against Larry Jansen. A very fine pitcher. We got a run in the first and a run in the second, but then Jansen retired sixteen in a row. I shut them out till the seventh when they got a run. Then in the last of the eighth we broke through on Jansen. We got a man on second and I drove him in with a single to center. That made it 3–1, which was the way it finished up.

That was another Series where certain writers said I didn't have a Chinaman's chance because the Giants were supposed to be murder on left-handers. When they interviewed me before the game and asked me about it I said, "Time will tell." What else can you say? So then when I beat the Giants in the Stadium the writers said no way could I do it in the Polo Grounds, because of the short foul lines. Even Stengel was a little skeptical. But when my turn came up again, in the fifth game, he started me in the Polo Grounds. Well, I pitched a good game, giving them only five hits and one run, which was unearned. But not too many people were noticing what I was doing because we buried the Giants, 13–1. Gil McDougald hit a grand slammer that day.

No, it didn't bother me what they were writing. I'd been in the game too many years by that time. I felt if I got nailed I got nailed, that's all, and if I did then it was just too bad. And as it turned out, I didn't get nailed. As a matter of fact, over the two games I gave them only ten hits and one earned run. Of the ten hits Monte Irvin got five, Al Dark got three, and the rest of the club got just two hits off of me in both games.

After I had beaten the Giants for the second time, some of the writers came up to me and said, "Well, you proved you could do it." I thought that was pretty funny. Here I'd been in the big leagues for eight years and been a winning pitcher most of the time and some people thought I still had to prove myself.

But that second game in 1951 wasn't all roses for me. It was kind of chilly that day and my arm started to tighten up in the seventh inning. I was thinking about getting out and Stengel talked to me about it. "Why don't you put your jacket on and let Kuzava finish up?" he said. I should have listened to him. Hell, we had the big lead. If it was anything but a World Series game I would have left. But I told him I'd stay in, which I did, and I finished strong. But when I got into the clubhouse I could hardly lift my arm. I had the feeling this might mean trouble.

I took some heat treatments over the next couple of days. Then I had the arm examined and the doctor told me I'd torn a tendon. That's when I started to get concerned. Hell, I was thirty-three years old and that's a bad time to start having arm problems. If I had left the game in the seventh inning I probably could have avoided all the trouble. Those last few innings were what hurt me. But there's that World Series magic again—you just don't want to come out of one of those games. When you hear a guy tell you how special the World Series is you'd better believe him. I should have known better than to stay in when I began feeling something wrong; in fact I did know better, but stayed all the same.

That arm bothered me for the next couple of years. I missed three months in '52 because of it. In the spring of '53 it was still bothering me and I took some X-ray therapy. It finally got to the point where I became a once-a-week pitcher. I started only twenty-four games. In spite of all the trouble I had one of my best years in 1953. I led the league in winning percentage and earned-run average. But if we'd have a long inning late in the game the arm would start to tighten and it would take me a while to crank it up. I'd tell Berra, "Get lost this inning." Yogi went and hid down in the runway while I warmed up with somebody else. I'd throw fifteen or twenty pitches to try and get loose again. The other manager would raise hell, and finally Yogi would come out on the field with some cock-and-bull story about having to fix his mitt or something.

Then one day a funny thing happened. It was late in the game and I was on first base and could feel the arm tightening. The batter got a base hit and I ran full blast to third, sliding in hard. When I went back out to the mound for the next inning my arm was just as loose as could be. I couldn't understand it. I talked to the trainer about it later and he said that the hard run probably stimulated my system and drove away the tightness. Well, from then on any time I hit a ball late in the game, even if it was a little pop-up, I'd run as hard as I could down the first base line and keep on running halfway out to right field, to keep that circulation going. It helped quite a bit. The fans must have thought I was a hell of a hustler.

In '52 we beat out Cleveland by two games and were back in the Series for the fourth straight year. By this time I had learned not to make any plans for the first week in October.

We played the Dodgers again that year and I didn't have a very good Series. Preacher Roe beat me 5–3 in the third game, at the Stadium. I'll tell you, that was a hell of a Dodger team. We hadn't seen them in a Series since '49. They were a lot more experienced now, with a very tough lineup. Every guy was a star—Reese, Furillo, Hodges, Robinson, Cox, Campanella, Pafko, Snider. We figured it was going to be a rough Series, and it was. It went seven games.

I started the seventh game. The day before, Raschi and Reynolds had worked. So when we got to the ball park we held a meeting. The decision was I would start but that everybody else would be standing by. Normally, Stengel didn't like to start me in Ebbets Field, much less in the seventh game, but he didn't have too many other choices that day.

I breezed along through the first three innings. But then in the fourth Snider opened with a single. Jackie Robinson beat out a bunt.

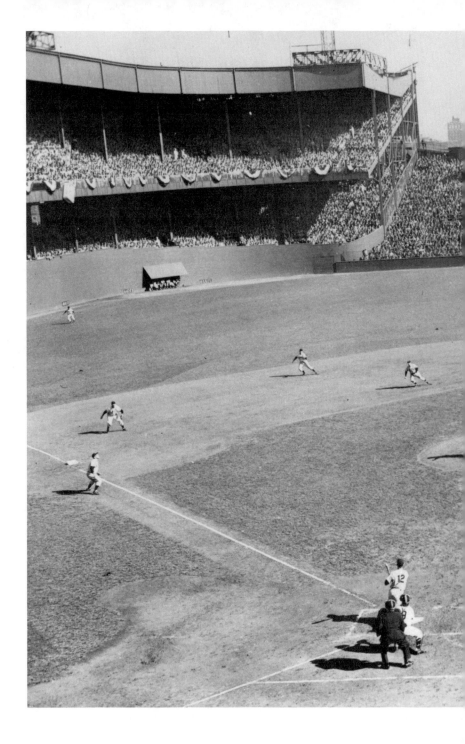

Gil McDougald unloading a grand slam home run at the Polo Grounds in the fifth game of the 1951 World Series.

That brought up Campanella. I yelled over to Gil McDougald at third to come in, that Campy was going to bunt. But Gil didn't believe me and stayed back. Sure enough, Campy laid one down the third base line. It wasn't a very good bunt, but because McDougald was back it went for a base hit. That loaded the bases with Hodges coming up. Stengel brought in Reynolds and Allie pitched out of it. Later on Raschi came in and then Bob Kuzava. Everybody chipped in. We beat the Dodgers 4–2. It was our fourth straight world championship.

When we all got together again the next spring we looked at each other and said, "Once more, huh?" Once more it was. And that proved to be the easiest one of all. We put together an eighteen-game streak in June and breezed home.

The Dodgers were back too, with that same strong team. Well, the newspapermen started up again. Casey said I'd be pitching the second game and right away the stories appeared in the papers as to how I'd started twice against the Dodgers the year before and been unable to finish either game. So I told myself I not only had to beat them a ball game but also go the nine. I was pretty darned determined about it.

In the last of the eighth, with the score tied 2–2, Mantle hit one out with a man on. So I had one more inning to go. But that Dodger team was tough to sink. In the top of the ninth they got two men on with two out and Duke Snider up. A guy who can wreck your ball game with one swing.

I'll never forget it. Berra came out to talk to me and then Stengel walked out and stood there with his arms folded, rocking back on his heels and looking at me.

"How ya feelin'?" he asked.

"All right," I said.

"Yog," he said to Berra, "how about it?"

"He's still all right," Yogi said.

"I got the big guy and the little guy ready," Stengel said. The big guy was Reynolds and the little guy was Ford. Two pretty good guys. "Now you're sure you're all right?"

"Case," I said, "how long have I been pitching for you?"

"Five years," he said.

"Have I ever lied to you?"

"No," he said.

"Well," I said, "you don't think I'm going to start now, do you?"

"Okay, Mr. Lopat," he said and walked away.

Then I looked at Snider standing there. I knew if I could get the ball away from him he'd hit it on the ground and I'd be okay. Well, I threw a fastball down away and he tried to pull it and hit a ground ball to Billy Martin at second. I watched Billy pick it up and throw it to first. The ball landed in Joe Collins' glove at first base and as I walked off the mound I said to myself, "Well, you finally went nine against the terrifying Dodgers."

Joe Wood in 1914

Joe Wood

JOSEPH WOOD

Born: October 25, 1889, Kansas City, Missouri
Major League career: 1908–1922, Boston Red Sox, Cleveland Indians
Lifetime record: 114 wins, 58 losses
Lifetime average: .283

An army injury suffered when Smoky Joe Wood was twenty-three years old curtailed what would unquestionably have been one of the greatest pitching careers in big league history. The year before the injury, 1912, Wood had what many consider the greatest single season ever enjoyed by a pitcher. He won 34 and lost 5, had 10 shutouts, 258 strikeouts, a 1.91 earned run average, and completed 35 of 38 starts. Wood capped off his remarkable season by winning three games against the Giants in the World Series.

A versatile and talented all-around ball player, Wood eventually switched to the outfield and in 1921 batted .366 for the Cleveland Indians.

THAT'S RIGHT, when I was a boy growing up there was no such thing as a World Series. The first World Series wasn't played until 1903, when I was fourteen years old. As a matter of fact, for a long time I didn't even know what the big leagues were. Didn't know about John McGraw or Honus Wagner or Christy Mathewson or any of those fellows. All I knew about baseball was what I was doing myself, which was playing on a town team in Ouray, Colorado. This was in 1903, '04, parts of '05.

Those people out in western Colorado were crazy about baseball. They used to have town teams and they'd cross the mountains to play each other. Everybody made a great hullabaloo out of those ball games. That was the center of it as far as we were concerned; we just didn't pay much attention to baseball anywhere else.

165

The first I heard about the World Series was when I got into professional ball with Hutchinson, Kansas. This was in 1907. I've got a very hazy recollection of hearing something about the Cubs and the Tigers. I seem to remember somebody talking about those great Chicago pitchers—Three Finger Brown, Orval Overall, Ed Reulbach, and that sharp little catcher they had, Johnny Kling, who was supposed to be one of the best ever. The Tigers had a young outfielder by the name of Ty Cobb. I heard his name mentioned. But I really didn't take much interest in the World Series.

I was born in Kansas City, Missouri, but soon after that we moved to Chicago and were there for ten years. Then my father got the gold fever and joined the Alaska gold rush. He spent some time there trying to make his fortune, same as a lot of other people. No, he didn't strike it rich. As a matter of fact he was lucky to get out alive. The Yukon River was frozen over, you see, and he had to walk out. He wrapped his feet up to his knees in gunnysacks and walked out, thirty miles a day. When he got out the doctors told him the only way he'd get the circulation and the feeling back in his legs was to go barefoot in the sand. So he went down to the gold strike in California and Nevada. The climate might have been better down there, but his luck stayed the same.

When he finally came home we got into a covered wagon and located way out in Ouray, Colorado. We were there for a few years, then came back to Kansas, then went on to the old family homestead in Pennsylvania. They talk about this being an on-the-go society today, what with the automobile and super highways and all that, but it seems to me that Americans were always a restless people. Back then those wagon wheels were always grinding, and wherever you went you met people going in the opposite direction.

But wherever I was I played baseball. That's all I lived for. When I sat up on the front seat of that covered wagon next to my father I was wearing a baseball glove. That showed anybody who was interested where *I* wanted to go.

I was a pretty good ball player, too. I could hit, I could run, and I could throw the ball hard. In 1908 I pitched for Kansas City in the

American Association, struck out a few fellows, and in August was sold to the Red Sox. I was eighteen years old then.

Cy Young was on that Red Sox team. He was around forty years old at the time, but I don't think you could say he was over the hill since he pitched 300 innings that year and won twenty-one games. No, he didn't pay much attention to me. I don't think we talked to one another at all. I was just an unknown kid coming onto the club. Sure, I knew who he was. By that time I had heard of them all, and Cy Young was the greatest pitcher of his day. I don't suppose there are many people alive today who saw him in his heyday, but for a long time it was said he was the greatest pitcher who ever lived. I don't know how you can measure those things; I guess each generation has its candidates for the greatest this or the greatest that. As far as I'm concerned, Walter Johnson was the greatest pitcher that ever lived. I just never saw anyone else who had as much natural ability. He could throw the ball by you so fast you never knew whether you'd swung under it or over it.

Tris Speaker was a kid outfielder on that Red Sox team in 1908. Somehow or other we got together and were roommates for fifteen

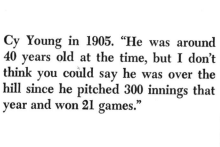

Cy Young in 1905. "He was around 40 years old at the time, but I don't think you could say he was over the hill since he pitched 300 innings that year and won 21 games."

years in the American League, with Boston and then later on with Cleveland. Among the men he played with and against, Speaker was always pretty much regarded as the best outfielder of all time. He simply did everything well. I don't think you could ask for a better all-around ball player.

As the years go by, some men naturally stand out sharper in memory than others. Cobb, of course. Nobody who watched him play could ever forget it. No, there was no way to pitch him except to throw him the best you had. But Cobb didn't give me near as much trouble as that other fellow they had, Sam Crawford. Sam was a big, strong hitter, and it was just tough trying to get the ball past him.

Lajoie was another top-notch player from those days. Some people called him Larry and some called him Napoleon. But whatever you called him, he could sock that ball! He drove a liner back at me one time that caught me in the leg and almost broke it in two. Great hitter. And graceful in the field. As graceful a ball player as I ever saw.

Ed Walsh got credit for being the greatest spitball pitcher there ever was. I guess he was the one who practically started it. But the fellow who threw the best-breaking spitter that I ever saw was Stanley Coveleski. Stanley and I were teammates on the Cleveland ball club that won the world championship in 1920, so I saw plenty of him. But you asked about Ed Walsh. Great, big, husky fellow, and a swell-looking guy. The year I came into the league he won forty games. That's four-oh. He used to come to Boston with the White Sox and pitch the first game and then like as not finish the next three. He was a workhorse. And never got paid for it. But of course nobody got very much money in those days, outside of Cobb and Speaker. The year I won thirty-four games I was getting something like four or five thousand, then had to battle like the devil to get seventy-five hundred the next year. How much would a thirty-four-game winner get paid today? I don't know. You tell me.

Rube Waddell was just leaving the league when I came in. He had had a great career, mostly with Connie Mack's A's, but he was with St. Louis when I knew him. He was still a fairly young man when he left baseball, maybe around thirty-two or thirty-three years old. He

Nap Lajoie. "Some people called him Larry and some called him Napoleon. But whatever you called him, he could sock that ball!"

told me that Eddie Cicotte hit him on the wrist with a ball and that that was what finished him. Eddie Cicotte was with the Red Sox when I joined them, you know. He was one of our regular starters for a few years, then he was traded to the White Sox and later became involved in that 1919 scandal. The Black Sox scandal. That included Shoeless Joe Jackson, if you recall. And what a pity it was. I always maintained you couldn't blame Joe for anything. He was not a very well-educated fellow; they said he couldn't read or write. I guess somebody talked him into that mess. But one of the greatest ball players of all time. What a hitter! He'd carry that big black bat up there and whale away. You just had to admire him, even though he might be beating your brains out. How did you pitch to him? Same as with Cobb—try your best and hope it isn't his day. Hitters like that—Jackson, Cobb, Speaker, Lajoie—there's no set way to pitch them. They don't have a weakness. Their averages bear that out, and I mean the consistency of those averages—year after year they're anywhere between .350 and .400. Just because you got them out on a certain pitch one time didn't mean they weren't going to whack that same pitch next time up.

Seems nowadays everybody is down at the end of the bat. That's one of the reasons you have so many strikeouts today. You saw very little of that when I was pitching. They choked up and just swung to meet the ball. It takes a natural hitter to go down to the end of the bat. Jackson could do it, and Crawford and Lajoie and Speaker. Not too many of them. Cobb, for instance. He was up on that bat.

Eddie Plank? Well, he was a different sort of pitcher than, say, Johnson or Waddell. They were power pitchers. Plank was very studious out there. He used to pitch to spots, more so than most fellows of the day I would say. They do that more today, but Eddie Plank was doing it back then, in the first decade of the century, and doing it very well. I'll say. He was a 300-game winner. Connie Mack's three mainstays in those years were Plank, Chief Bender and Jack Coombs. Coombs was a thirty-game winner for Mr. Mack one year. He wasn't too fast but he had a big, beautiful curve ball. But it seemed to be that whenever Connie Mack had a very important game on, a game that meant a lot, Chief Bender was the pitcher. They had Bullet Joe Bush too in those days. I was Smoky Joe and he was Bullet Joe. I guess we both could throw the ball pretty fast.

The Philadelphia Athletics had great teams in those years. In fact,

Chief Bender. "But it seemed to be that whenever Connie Mack had a very important game on ... Chief Bender was the pitcher."

Eddie Plank. "... very studious out there."

between 1910 and 1914 the only team to beat them out of a pennant was the Red Sox in '12.

In 1911 we finished fifth. All the same, when we got together for spring training in Hot Springs, Arkansas, the next year we had pennant on our minds. Jake Stahl had taken over as player-manager and he kept us on our toes. We won it by fourteen games, never letting up for a second. We went with a three-man rotation most of the time—Hugh Bedient, Buck O'Brien, and myself. The games we didn't start, Charley Hall and Ray Collins did. And everybody was ready to relieve, too, if need be. We'd get in a tough game going into the late innings and two or three of the fellows would come over to me and say, "How about it, Woodie?" And I'd go down in the corner and start throwing and be ready to go in. You see, today relief pitching is an art. The brigade heads down to the bull pen before the game starts. It wasn't like that back then. Nobody went down there until the middle of the game. There was no such thing as a relief specialist. You started and you relieved, you relieved and you started.

We won one hundred and five games that year, which was an American League record at the time. The five of us—Bedient, O'Brien, Hall, Collins, and myself—won one hundred and two of the one hundred

Joe Bush. "I was Smoky Joe and he was Bullet Joe."

and five games. That was the year I had my best record—thirty-four wins and five losses. Put together a sixteen-game win streak along the way. I was just twenty-two years old at the time, and as far as I was concerned still hadn't reached my peak.

I'd say that was quite a good team we had in Boston in 1912. In the infield we had Jake Stahl, Heinie Wagner, Steve Yerkes, and at third base one of the best, Larry Gardner. And we had three fellows in the outfield they're still talking about today: Harry Hooper, Tris Speaker and Duffy Lewis. Best defensive outfield ever. Bill Carrigan and Hick Cady were the catchers.

By the time September rolled around there was no question but that we were going to win the pennant. We just kept charging along, all keyed up. I was winning ball games wholesale and I suppose I was getting a lot of attention in the newspapers. Well, that seemed to upset somebody because I got a couple of threatening letters in the middle of September. I found one waiting for me in Cleveland and another in Detroit. Both from the same person and both with pretty much the same message: I would soon be no more. Sure, we had crackpots in those days, same as you have today. No, I didn't take it seriously. Maybe I should have, but I didn't. I think the only one I showed the letters to was Speaker. We just laughed them off and forgot about the whole thing. Nothing ever came of it.

That was the year Fenway Park opened, so you might say we got it off to a good start. There was plenty of excitement over that World Series. The Red Sox had a contingent of fans called the Royal Rooters. And they were just that. The most fanatical fans you could imagine. They had their own band and would parade on the field before a game. I'll tell you something about that Series. We played the Giants and the games alternated between New York and Boston. It was a seven-game Series and it was one day in New York, one day in Boston, and so on. Well, the Royal Rooters went back and forth on the train with us. So we didn't get much rest on the train rides because they were a noisy bunch; loyal and good-natured as all get-out, but noisy.

There was a good deal of excitement in New York too for that Series. We were staying at a hotel called Bretton Hall, which was uptown on

Broadway, and when we went from the hotel out to the ball park we had to keep the blinds down in the taxicabs, otherwise we'd get pelted with rocks.

John McGraw had a good, tough ball club that year. I guess all of McGraw's teams of that era were good ones. They'd won the pennant the year before and they were going to win it again the next year. I would say they were probably the most famous team in baseball. I mean, people who didn't know anything about baseball might have heard of John McGraw and the Giants, just like years later they heard of Babe Ruth and the Yankees. And of course McGraw's most famous player was Christy Mathewson. Another candidate for greatest pitcher ever.

Mathewson wasn't a kid any longer by the time we got into the '12 Series. He was nearing the end of the trail, but still a great pitcher. I don't think he was as fast as he had once been. When I saw him his greatest asset was control and a beautiful curve ball that he'd start over your head and bring right down. I'd never seen a curve ball like it. He also threw what they called the fadeaway, which is the same as a screwball. As far as I know, he was the only one who threw it at that time.

Let's see who else I can remember from that Giant team. They had Larry Doyle, Fred Merkle, Chief Meyers catching, Buck Herzog, Art Fletcher, Fred Snodgrass, Red Murray, Josh Devore. That was a good, sharp ball club.

I knew I was going to get the first game in the Series. There was no question about my starting it off. I may not have heard about the World Series before, but I sure knew what it was now. When I went out to warm up that day at the Polo Grounds there were about 35,000 people sitting in the stands. I guess I felt a little extra pressure, but as quick as the game started it was gone. I think most ball players will tell you the same thing—they feel the special excitement of the World Series, but only until the first pitch is thrown, that first good fastball. That's right, I was primarily a fastball pitcher. I had a good curve too. Fastball and curve. That's all there was to it. Didn't throw anything else.

A crowded grandstand at the Polo Grounds watching the 1912 World Series

I started against Jeff Tesreau. In fact, I started three times in that Series and each time against Jeff Tesreau. I don't know why McGraw picked him over Mathewson to open. They also had Rube Marquard. But Tesreau was a good pitcher. He threw the spitball.

I was throwing hard that day, very hard. I struck out eleven. But even so, going into the top of the seventh I was down 2–1. In the last of the third the Giants had men on second and third with two out and Red Murray hit one into center to score them.

But then we got three runs in the seventh. Harry Hooper got a big hit in that inning and Steve Yerkes knocked in two runs with a hit. I didn't have any trouble in the seventh and eighth, but in the bottom of the ninth the Giants really threw a scare.

That last half of the ninth inning was quite a thrill for me. The Giants scored one run and had men on second and third with one out. The tying and winning runs. Art Fletcher was up. Same fellow who later coached on the Yankees under McCarthy. Well, I threw so hard I thought my arm would fly right off my body. I struck Fletcher out. That was two out and the fellows in the infield were yelling, "One more, Woodie." The batter was Doc Crandall. He had come in to relieve Tesreau. Crandall was a hard hitter and McGraw let him bat. One thing I was tickled to death about was that McGraw didn't use Beals Becker as a pinch hitter in that spot. Becker was sitting right there on the bench, and I was kind of looking out of the corner of my eye to see if he would get up. You see, I had played against him in the Western Association and he had always hit me pretty well. But I guess McGraw didn't know that.

I ran the count on Crandall to three and two. Fastballs, that's what I was throwing. Just burning them in and hoping for the best. Well, on the full-count pitch I threw one right on by him for strike three. That was the biggest thrill I ever had in baseball, those two strikeouts.

Jeff Tesreau

After pitching the opener I came back with only two days rest. I don't know why Stahl did that, he had those other starters. But it never bothered me any. I won both of those games. The score of the second one was 3–1 and I knocked in the third one myself with a base hit in the ninth inning. Say, I could swing the bat. After I hurt my arm I turned to the outfield and one year hit .366 for Cleveland. I took a lot of pride in that. As I said to somebody once, I was a *ball player*, not just a pitcher.

Then Hugh Bedient beat Mathewson 2–1 in Boston and we had them down three games to one. So it looked pretty good for us. But as I said, McGraw had a lot of first-rate players and they didn't quit; they came right back at us. Marquard beat O'Brien in the fifth game. O'Brien gave up five runs in the first inning and that was the ball game. Marquard beat us 5–2. You don't spot a pitcher like Rube Marquard five runs in the first inning and then expect to enjoy your dinner that night.

After the game, which was played in New York, we hopped the train back to Boston. Later on a story came out that said there had been an argument on the train between Jake Stahl and Jim McAleer, who owned the team, over who the starting pitcher should have been for that game. According to the story, Jake wanted to start me with two days' rest again but McAleer had insisted on O'Brien. Then another story had my brother having a fight with O'Brien on the train. Well, there wasn't a word of truth in any of it. It was absolutely false. How those stories get started I'll never know.

So I had three days' rest before my next start—and gave up six runs in the first inning! I was out of there before I knew what was happening. You know, there was a big ruckus just before the game. It seems that more tickets had been sold than there were seats, and it so happened that the people who were shut out were the Royal Rooters. Well, it took the mounted police to get them to go and when they finally did go they took part of the center-field fence with them. I was all warmed up and ready to start pitching and then that crowd broke down the fence. I had to go and sit down on the bench until it was fixed. Some people said that was why I got hit so hard in the first inning, that I had cooled off. But I don't think that had anything to do with it. I wasn't looking for any excuses. It was just one of those times when I couldn't get the ball by anybody. That would happen once in a while. Now and then there just wasn't anything on the fastball. Maybe two or three times a year it would happen. Not a darn thing you could do about it.

After the first inning we had little hope of catching up and the Giants ran away with it, 11–4. That tied the Series at three apiece. So there was going to be a seventh game. Actually it was the eighth game because one of the earlier games had ended in a tie because of darkness. But whatever number you want to call it, it was still the one that was going to decide everything.

That game has gone down in history as one of the most memorable ever played in a World Series. Things happened that day that are just as clear in my memory as this morning's breakfast. Mathewson, for instance. I can still see him and I can still hear him out there, making the most curious mistake in judgment for an experienced player. Sure he was the pitcher. That added to it. When you've got a Mathewson involved, or a Babe Ruth, or a Walter Johnson, that just adds to it.

Bedient started for us and Mathewson for them. They both pitched wonderfully well. Going into the bottom of the seventh—the game was played in Boston—we were losing 1–0. Then in the bottom of the seventh we put men on first and second with two out. Olaf Henriksen went up to hit for Bedient. It was Henriksen's one and only at bat in the Series. But he sure made it a good one—he banged out a double and tied the score.

They brought me on in the eighth. Against Mathewson. I don't know if I had any butterflies—it's a long time ago—but let's say I was definitely *impressed* by the situation. Not only is it the last game of the World Series and it's all tied up, but there's Christy Mathewson out there for the other side, and pitching just beautifully.

I held them in the eighth and ninth, but Mathewson stayed right with me. Then in the top of the tenth they scored a run. Red Murray doubled. Then Fred Merkle singled to score him, and when Speaker juggled the ball in center field Merkle went to second. I struck out

Red Murray, one of McGraw's
stalwarts

Buck Herzog. Then Chief Meyers hit one back at me a mile a minute.
I threw my bare hand out and the ball hit me on the wrist. I picked up
the ball and got Meyers at first. That was three out. If I hadn't
knocked down that shot and gotten Chief Meyers they would have
scored another run and how many more we'll never know. But I knew
I wasn't going to pitch anymore that day no matter what, because my
hand started to swell up even before I reached the bench.

So we're into the bottom of the tenth down by a run, 2–1, with
Christy Mathewson standing out there looking down our throats.

I was first up and ordinarily I would have batted for myself, but
because of that injured hand I couldn't swing a bat. So they sent
Clyde Engle up to bat for me. Clyde hit a soft fly ball out to Fred
Snodgrass in center. Snodgrass dropped it. Maybe once a year a man
would drop a ball like that. I'd seen it happen to Speaker, to Hooper,
to all of them. No reason. It just happens. The ball hits your glove and
falls out and that's all there is to it. If it happens in the middle of the
season it's forgotten the next day. But in a World Series, and in particular *that* kind of situation, well, here we are, sixty-six years later,
still talking about it.

Poor Fred Snodgrass. He'll always be remembered as the goat of that Series. But he didn't deserve it. What everybody forgets is that the next batter, Hooper, hit a real shot out to center and Snodgrass made a great catch of it. Nobody remembers that, but it was an outstanding play. Engle tagged up after the catch and went to third. Then Steve Yerkes got a walk and we've got men on first and third with Speaker up.

Then we got another break. This was the one that all of our fellows claimed was the turning point, more so than the dropped fly ball. What happened was, Speaker lifted a little pop foul between first and home. The first baseman, Fred Merkle, had the best shot at it. But instead of calling for Merkle to take it, Mathewson came down off the mound calling for Chief Meyers, the catcher. Merkle could have caught it easily, but Mathewson kept calling for Meyers, I'll never know why. You see, Merkle was coming in on the ball and the Chief was going with it. It's a much easier play for Merkle. But there was Matty, yelling for the Chief. I can hear him to this day. But Meyers never could get to it. The ball dropped. It just clunked down into the grass in foul ground and lay there. We couldn't believe it. Neither could Mathewson. You never saw a man as mad as he was when that ball hit the ground. But the way we saw it, it was his own fault. He called for the wrong man.

That's what we always felt won the Series for us. The write-ups in the papers never stressed that as much as they did Snodgrass dropping the ball in center field.

So Speaker had another shot, and you just can't do that with a hitter like Tris. Sure enough, he hit the next one into right field to tie the game. On the throw home the runners went to second and third. Duffy Lewis was next, but McGraw walked him to load the bases. That brought up Larry Gardner. Still just one out, remember. Larry was always a dependable fellow and he didn't disappoint us. He hit a long fly ball to right field to bring home Yerkes with the winning run —the world championship run.

I didn't realize it until later, what with all the excitement, but I was the winning pitcher in that game. It gave me three wins in the Series.

It topped off a swell season for me. The winner's share in that Series came to $4024.70. Sure I remember the amount. Hell, it was just about equal to my whole year's salary.

So there I was, a thirty-four-game winner, three more in the Series, and a world championship. And not yet twenty-three years old. It sure looked like riding the rainbow for a long time. But I was quite unfortunate when it came to mishaps. For instance, one time we were monkeying around in the room, Speaker and I, and he slammed the door on my toe and broke it. Another time I got hit with a ball in batting practice that caused a blood clot in my foot and I had to have an operation to get it out. Things like that.

I hurt my arm the following spring and it was never the same again. I lost something on my fastball. It never came back. I could still pitch now and then—in 1915 I won fifteen games and led the league in earned run average—but I couldn't pitch more than every two weeks or so because of the pain in my arm after each game. The pity of it was that over the next half-dozen years the Red Sox were the best team in the league—they won pennants in '15, '16, and '18. No telling how many games I could have won with those teams.

But it's all a long time ago now, isn't it? It's funny how some things stand out and others fade away. I think it was around 1908 when I was warming up on the sideline and a sports reporter for the Boston

Tris Speaker

Joe Wood (left) and Christy Mathewson during the 1912 World Series

Post named Paul Shannon was watching me. He turned to somebody and said, "That kid sure throws smoke." That was the origin of the nickname. It doesn't take much to get a nickname in baseball and once you've got it you might as well forget about ever getting rid of it. I'm eighty-eighty years old now and people still call me Smoky Joe. But that's all right. I don't mind.

Bill Hallahan

WILLIAM ANTHONY HALLAHAN

Born: August 4, 1902, Binghamton, New York
Major League career: 1925–1926, 1929–1938, St. Louis Cardinals, Cincinnati Reds, Philadelphia Phillies
Lifetime record: 102 wins, 94 losses

Possessor of a sizzling fastball, Bill Hallahan was a National League standout in the early 1930's. In 1931 he led the league's pitchers in wins with 19 and in '30 and '31 led also in strikeouts. Hallahan was particularly outstanding in the World Series' of 1930 and 1931, in each of those years pitching shutouts against the powerful Philadelphia Athletics. Over four World Series' his record stands at 3–1 and his earned run average of 1.36 is one of the lowest in Series history.

WELL, YOU just never know what's going to happen when you decide to try and make a career of baseball. I heard a story once about Connie Mack. As a young man Connie had the opportunity to play professional baseball. He mentioned this to his father, who said, "I guess it's all right; but why don't you get into something that's lasting?" This was in 1884. Connie stayed in the game until 1950. Sixty-six years. So you never know. It can be a year or ten years or twenty or fifty. Or it can be a few weeks, sometimes just one game. And then there are the fellows who give their all in spring training only to be handed the pink slip and sent off on that lonesome trip home.

I was satisfied with my career. I put in twelve years and some of them were very rewarding. I played on four pennant winners with the Cardinals and three world championship teams. One nice thing about baseball is that, generally, you're remembered for the successes you had rather than the failures, unless those failures are of themselves

Walter Johnson, left,
and Connie Mack

memorable. I never had any memorable failures, and I'm grateful
for that.

I always wanted to be a ball player. I guess most every kid does at
one time or another. I was a New York Giant fan and hoped that one
day I would be able to play for them. As a matter of fact, when I
was pitching in the Texas League in 1928 I was told that John Mc-
Graw was thinking of buying my contract from the Cardinals, but that

instead he decided to go for another left-hander who was also in the league that year—Carl Hubbell. Detroit had owned Hubbell for a few years and then let him go. When I pitched against Carl in the Texas League he was just beginning to develop that screwball. If Detroit had been patient just another year or two I doubt if they would have ever let him go. I guess most every team has had that sort of thing happen to them at one time or another. But when you lose a pitcher like Hubbell you stay haunted for a long time.

I grew up in Binghamton, New York. Oh yes, it was a baseball-minded community. Very much so. I would imagine most small communities in the country were at that time. This was before radio and television, remember, so our baseball seemed very important to us. When you don't have the big leaguers on your TV all the time your own kids on the sandlots seem a lot better and a lot more interesting.

World Series time was like a holiday, of course. I can remember going to the state armory to "watch" the games. Some local promoter rented the place and hooked up a wire that provided the play-by-play information. They had a big board with lights on it, in the batter's box and on each base. When somebody hit the ball the light would move to first base; if it stayed lit then you knew the batter had reached base safely, but if it went off then you knew the batter had made out. Anytime a man got on safely there was a light on that base. Pretty primitive by today's standards, isn't it? But that was the best we could do and at the time we thought it was exciting.

The game that stands out in my mind most was in the 1920 Series, when Brooklyn was playing Cleveland. The Dodgers had the bases loaded and all of a sudden all the lights seemed to blow out. There was a lot of confusion and nobody knew what happened, until finally some fellow came out on the stage and explained that Bill Wambsganss of Cleveland had just made an unassisted triple play. It had all happened so fast the lights just weren't able to keep up with it.

When we wanted to get the results of the games during the season we had to sneak into the taverns. Each tavern had a big scorecard that showed the line scores of the day's games. It was a service that they subscribed to from the newspapers, who got the results over the wire and then sent men around to the various taverns to drop off the scorecards. It was something the taverns did for their customers, and it was also an inducement to get people in there, much like the installation of TV sets in taverns in the early days of television. So if you wanted to see how your team had done that day you had to sneak in and get a peek at the cards. The trick was to get in there and slip up to the bar where the cards used to lay before the bartender saw you. They didn't like kids ducking in and out of the place and would really send up a roar when they saw us.

We had our heroes, but the pity was we could never see them. If you didn't live in or near a big league town in those days you just never had the opportunity to a game. So all the years I was growing up and my idols were players like Christy Mathewson and Honus Wagner, I never saw them play. What a great thing it is today for the kids, to just flick on the TV and see the big leaguers.

I was fortunate, though, to become a teammate of one of my boyhood heroes—Grover Cleveland Alexander. I was a rookie on the Cardinals in 1926 when we bought Alec from the Cubs in midseason. I'll never forget the first time he pitched for us. I was sitting on the bench with another young pitcher and naturally we glued our eyes on Alec when he went out to warm up. He flipped a few in to the catcher, then stopped, put his glove under his arm, took out a piece of chewing gum, very casually took the paper off, put the gum in his mouth, looked around through the stands, then put his glove back on and started throwing again. He threw just a few more pitches, very easily, with no effort. Then he was through. He came back to the bench, put on his sweater—we wore those big, red-knit sweaters on the Cardinals —and sat down.

I looked at this other fellow and said, "This is going to be murder. He isn't throwing *anything*." Well, Alec went out that day and stood the other team on its ear. Control, that's how he did it. Absolute, total control. He had this little screwball that he could turn over on the corners all day long. Amazing fellow. Born to be a pitcher.

No, I never talked pitching with him. Alec never said much about anything. When he did talk it was seldom above a whisper. As a rule

Bill Hallahan in 1930

you didn't see him around after a game. He was a loner. He would go off by himself and do what he did, which I suppose was drink. That was his problem. But he was a good-natured fellow. You never heard him say anything against anybody.

He liked to go out before a game and work in the infield, generally around third base. One day we were taking batting practice and there's Alec standing at third, crouched over, hands on knees, staring into the plate. A ground ball went by him and he never budged, just remained there stock still, staring in at the batter. Then another grounder buzzed by and same thing—he never moved a muscle. Then somebody ripped a line drive past his ear and still he didn't move. That's when Hornsby noticed him—Rog was managing the club at the time.

Hornsby let out a howl and said, "Where in the hell did he get it?" —Meaning the booze, of course. "Get him out of there before he gets killed."

So one of the coaches, Bill Killefer, I think, went out and brought Alec in and sat him on the bench. Hornsby was fuming. "Where did he get it? Where did he get it?" he kept yelling. He ordered a search made and they found it all right. In old Sportsman's Park in St. Louis there used to be a ladies' room not far from the corridor going down to the dugout, and that's where he had stashed it, up in the rafters of the ladies' room. One of those little square bottles of gin.

We won the pennant by just two games in 1930. Beat out Chicago. I pitched the game that was probably my best ever in Brooklyn right at the end of the season. At least that's what a lot of people think. I'll never forget that one, and for plenty of reasons.

We finished a series at the Polo Grounds against the Giants and went over to play the Dodgers. I think we were a half game out of first place. The night before I was going to pitch, I went out with Ray Blades and another fellow to see a show on Broadway. When we came out of the theater we figured we would take a cab back to the hotel. We hailed a cab and Ray got in first and I followed him. Then the other fellow jumped in, and when he did he pulled the door in with him, very quickly. Well, somehow that door closed right across the fingers of my right hand.

When we got back to the hotel the hand was killing me. And here I've got to pitch an important ball game the next day. The only lucky thing was it was my right hand and not my left. But all the same, when a door slams on your hand it hurts just as much whether it's the right one or the left. So when I went up to my room they sent our trainer, Doc Weaver, in to work on me. He sat up most of the night with me, applying hot and cold packs and massaging my arm. Branch Rickey, who was our general manager at the time, came into the room and asked me if I thought I would be able to pitch the next day.

"I pitch with my left hand, Mr. Rickey," I said.

Well, I've got to tell you what else was going on at the same time. It became one of those stories they're still talking about to this day. Sometime late that night somebody noticed that my roommate, Flint Rhem, hadn't shown up. Do you know about Flint? Well, he was a pitcher and a pretty good one too. But he had the same problem Alec did—a fondness for the booze. He was a very nice fellow, but now and then he did some strange things.

Flint never did show up that night, nor did he show up the next night either. When he finally did reappear the reporters asked him where he'd been. Flint kind of hemmed and hawed, until one of the reporters jokingly asked him if he had been kidnapped.

You could see Flint think about it for a minute, and then he said, "That's right. I was kidnapped by some gamblers who wanted to make sure I didn't pitch." Hell, he wasn't even scheduled to pitch.

"Is that so?" somebody asked.

Flint Rhem. "He was a very nice fellow, but now and then he did some strange things."

"That's right," Flint said. He was really getting warmed up now. "They kidnapped me and took me to a room someplace. Then they held a gun to my head and made me keep drinking whiskey until I passed out."

That was the best part of the story, and one of the writers remarked in the paper the next day: "Imagine kidnapping Flint Rhem and *forcing* him to drink whiskey?"

What happened, we found out later, was some friends of Flint's had come up from South Carolina to see the games in New York and Brooklyn. After the games in the Polo Grounds they went out for a few drinks and just kept going.

Meanwhile, I was having my own troubles. I was still in considerable pain the next morning. But there was never any doubt in my mind that I was going to pitch. It was an important game and I wanted to be in it. Two fingers on my right hand were packed in some sort of black salve and I had to cut my glove so they could protrude on the outside.

Dazzy Vance started for the Dodgers and he was really firing that day. But so was I. I had a no-hitter until the eighth inning. At one point I retired twenty in a row. At the end of nine there was no score. In the top of the tenth we got a run on a couple of hits by Andy High and Taylor Douthit. In the bottom of the tenth the Dodgers gave us a scare. They loaded the bases with one out. Then Al Lopez hit a ground ball to Sparky Adams at short. Sparky threw to Frisch at second and Frank made the fastest pivot I ever saw in my life and we just did nip Lopez at first. There was a full house in Ebbets Field that day and the crowd was just stunned, absolutely stunned. You didn't hear a sound.

I would say it was probably my best game, and not just because I pitched well but because it meant so much. We were right at the end of the season and really needed that one.

You had to be at the top of your game to beat Vance. When Dazzy had his stuff he was almost unhittable. He was one of the greatest pitchers I ever saw. He could throw hard. And he had an exceptional curve, too. I saw many a right-handed hitter fall away from that curve and then be highly embarrassed when it was called a strike.

I got to know Dazzy very well later on. He joined the Cardinals at the end of his career and was with us when we won the World Series in 1934. I remember a group of us went out to a Greek restaurant in St. Louis to celebrate the victory. Dazzy decided he would mix the drinks. The owner of the place let him go behind the bar and Dazzy got a big glass and poured a little bit from just about every bottle into it. Then he brought it over to the table and said it was the "Dazz-marine Special." He offered the glass around the table, but nobody would touch it. So he downed the whole thing himself. He was prac-

Dazzy Vance. " 'All the chairs in the lobby,' he said. 'They're jumping at me.' "

tically kayoed on the spot. Later, when we were helping him across the hotel lobby, he suddenly stopped and took hold of our arms and really squeezed tight.

"Stop boys," he said. "Wait a minute."

"What's wrong, Daz?" we asked.

"Don't you see it?" he said.

"See what?"

"All the chairs in the lobby," he said. "They're jumping at me."

Dazzy wouldn't move until Joe Medwick, who was with us, walked ahead and told Vance he wouldn't let the chairs get at him.

Dazzy was always a great character. When he was with Brooklyn he loved to play tricks on his manager, Uncle Wilbert Robinson, who was a lovable and gullible old man. One time somebody hit a scorcher passed Chick Fewster, the second baseman. It was a low line drive that went out there like a pistol shot, as sudden a base hit as you'd want to see. Vance was in the dugout and he turned to the fellow sitting next to him and, just loud enough for Uncle Robbie to hear, said, "What's the matter with Fewster? He didn't even move on that ball."

So when the inning was over and Fewster came into the dugout, Uncle Robbie said to him, "Say, Chick, what happened on that ball? Why didn't you pick it up?"

Fewster was ready to explode, but then he looked around and saw Dazzy sitting there with a big grin and knew what had happened.

It's hard to believe today what an unusual personality Uncle Robbie was. I remember coming out of Ebbets Field after a game one day and there he was, talking to a group of cab drivers, explaining to them what had happened in the game and giving the reasons for his strategy. Can you imagine a manager doing that today?

Dizzy Dean was another colorful one. I guess I don't have to tell you that. In the '34 Series he and his brother Paul won two games apiece to beat the Tigers—just as Dizzy had said they would. There was one game in that Series when Dizzy went in as a pinch runner. Frisch, who was managing the club then, has received a lot of criticism for putting a thirty-game winner in to pinch-run. Well, here's how

Dizzy Dean, pinch runner, getting hit in the head in the 1934 World Series. Second baseman Charlie Gehringer is at the right, shortstop Billy Rogell in the middle.

it happened. We needed somebody to run, and while Frisch was looking up and down the bench trying to decide who to put in, Diz ran out there, on his own. Somebody said to Frisch, "Dizzy's already out there." Frisch took a look and sure enough, there was Dean, standing on first base. Frisch frowned; he didn't like the idea. But the guy was already on the field, so he said, "Okay, let him be." Wouldn't you know it, but the batter hits the ball to Charley Gehringer at second, who picks it up and flips to Billy Rogell, who crosses the bag and cocks his arm to throw to first for the double play, and here's Diz coming in standing up. Well, Rogell threw it all right. *Pow!* The relay hit Dean right in the head and he went down like he'd been shot. We all stood up in the dugout and you could just feel what everybody was thinking: there goes the Series.

They carried Diz off the field and carted him away to the hospital. That night Diz came into the hotel with a big grin on his face and told everybody, "It's okay. They X-rayed my head and didn't find anything."

But that's how it happened. There was no way Frisch would have sent him in to run. No sir. You don't do that with thirty-game winners.

You know, there was a funny thing after the second game in Detroit. We lost it, and after the game our team bus got a big police escort back to the hotel, with motorcycles and blaring sirens. But when we *won* in Detroit, it was, "Get back the best way you can. You're on your own."

In the 1930 World Series we went up against one of the greatest teams of all time—the Philadelphia Athletics. Jimmie Foxx, Al Simmons, Mickey Cochrane, Mule Haas, Bing Miller, Max Bishop, and so on. Not to mention three of the best pitchers you'll ever want to see on one staff—Lefty Grove, George Earnshaw, and Rube Walberg.

But we had a pretty good outfit ourselves. This might be hard to believe, but every man in our starting lineup hit better than .300. There was Jim Bottomley, Frisch, Charlie Gelbert, Sparky Adams, Chick Hafey, Taylor Douthit, George Watkins, and Jimmie Wilson. Those were the regulars. In addition, we had men on the bench hitting better than .300—Ray Blades, Gus Mancuso, Showboat Fischer, Ernie Orsatti. Overall the team hit around .314.

We ran up against Grove and Earnshaw in the first two games and lost. I started the third game and drew Rube Walberg. I had a rugged first inning. They filled the bases with two out and Bing Miller came up. He was a very tough hitter. As a matter of fact, they didn't have a soft spot in their lineup either. I went to a full count on Miller and I can remember standing out there on the mound rubbing up the ball and thinking to myself, "Well, what do you do when you've run the count full and the bases are loaded?" The answer was easy: you put everything you've got on the ball and hope he doesn't hit it. That's just what happened. Miller was one of the most deadly curve ball hitters that ever lived. So I threw him my best fastball and he swung and missed. I went on from there to pitch a shutout, which was a pretty good trick against that team.

I was basically a fastball pitcher, but every now and then I would change speeds a little. You just can't throw every pitch as hard as you can for nine innings. But, gee, every time I did that I would hear one of my infielders, Frisch or somebody, start yelling, "Bear

Two 30-game winners shake hands before the 1936 All-Star game. Lefty Grove, on the left, and Dizzy Dean.

down! Bear down!" I remember Frisch hollering at me during that World Series, "Stop experimenting out there! Who do you think you are—Thomas Edison?"

Well, they came back to beat us in six games. Grove and Earnshaw each won two. That was the second straight world championship for them and people were saying that nobody was going to be able to stop that team for years to come. They sure were a great team, but we had a secret weapon waiting for them when we played them in the Series again the next year. The name of the weapon was Pepper Martin.

That was Pepper's first full year with us. He showed up well, too, hitting around .300 and proving to be a real hustler. A good ball player all right, but then came the Series in 1931 and he just tore it apart. He got twelve hits, hit .500, caught everything in sight in center field, and the thing that people remember most, stole five bases. Another thing about his record in that Series, and I don't imagine a lot of people realize this, is that Pepper did all of his hitting in the first five games. In other words, he went twelve for eighteen until they finally stopped him in the last two games. Now and then individual players have taken charge of a World Series, but I don't think anyone ever did it as dramatically or as colorfully as Pepper did in 1931. What he did in that one week caught the fancy of fans all over the country and established his reputation forever.

Mickey Cochrane, the A's catcher, got a lot of criticism for letting Pepper steal so many bases. But that was nonsense, of course. We ball players knew that. Pepper was stealing on the pitchers—most bases are stolen on the pitcher. He stole all of his bases against Grove and Earnshaw because those fellows just didn't hold a runner on very well. You give a catcher like Cochrane a chance to throw you out and he's going to do it. Nobody can outrun a ball.

The Series didn't start too well for us. We opened with Paul Derringer and the A's hit him hard. They beat us 6–2.

I started the second game against Earnshaw. George had beaten me just a year before, but this time I got the edge. I shut them out, 2–0. Pepper had a hand in both runs, or I should say he had his feet

Eddie Collins. ". . . as sharp a baseball man as ever lived."

in both runs. He doubled with one out in the second and then the son of a gun stole third and scored on Jimmie Wilson's fly ball. Later in the game he singled, stole second and came around on a ground ball and a squeeze play.

I went into the ninth up by those two runs and experienced an inning I'll never forget as long as I live. Jimmie Foxx led off and I walked him. Then Bing Miller flied out. I walked Jimmie Dykes. I got a called third strike by Dib Williams. Then Connie Mack sent up a fellow named Jim Moore to pinch-hit for Earnshaw. Well, I got two strikes on him and then broke off a beauty of a curve and he struck out on it. Or so I thought. It was a low pitch and Jimmie Wilson caught it right down on the ground, figured it was strike three and for some reason fired it down to third base to Jake Flowers, thinking the game was over. I don't know why in the world he did that; maybe it was some sort of reflex.

Eddie Collins was coaching first base for the A's. He started hollering at Moore to run to first base—Moore had already turned to start back to the dugout. So Moore ran to first base and the other two runners moved up. We didn't know what was going on. Jake Flowers was just standing there with the ball in his hand. You see, the umpire ruled that Wilson had scooped up the third strike—the ball had hit the ground first—and in that particular situation you have to put the batter out at first base, or tag him, if you can. Eddie Collins, who was as sharp a baseball man as ever lived, was the only one who realized what had happened, and that's why he yelled at Moore to run.

You know, Flowers came up to me later and said he nearly threw the ball into the stands, that it had been his impulse to do so. That would have been great—all three runs would have scored, or at least two of them anyway. Can you imagine two or three runs scoring on a strikeout? Well, it nearly happened. Then Jake said he thought that maybe I would want that ball as a memento. Memento heck; I needed that ball back to get the next man out with.

I already had some of the infielders patting me on the back and saying "Nice game." The outfielders were running in. But then somebody told us to get back there, that the man was safe and the bases were loaded.

There was an argument, of course, which we lost, of course. So I had to go back onto the mound and do it again. You don't like to give a team like the A's four outs in an inning, but that's what I had to do. The batter was Max Bishop, a fellow I didn't like to pitch to. He was a smart little hitter who generally got the bat on the ball. I always preferred working to the big free-swingers because they gave you a lot of pitching room, the way they wound up with those bats. But a fellow like Bishop—they called him "Camera Eye"—guarded the plate like a hawk and it was hard to get a ball past him.

I put everything I had on it and Bishop popped one up in foul ground that Jim Bottomley chased down and then dove over the Athletics' bull pen bench and caught by reaching into the stands. It was a really remarkable play by Jim. That ended the game for real. I always said it was a lucky thing we were playing at home, because the fans got out of the way and let Jim make the play. If we had been in Philadelphia I'm sure they wouldn't have been so helpful.

We won the next day with Burleigh Grimes and then lost the next

Two Philadelphia fence-busters: Chuck Klein of the Phillies, left, and Jimmie Foxx of the Athletics.

one. In that fourth game Jimmie Foxx hit a home run over the left-field pavilion that was hit just as hard and as far as any ball I've ever seen. One of our bull pen pitchers, Jim Lindsey, said later, "We were watching that ball for two innings."

I started the fifth game, against Waite Hoyt. I beat them 5–1, and again I had a little help from Pepper. Just a little. All he did was drive in one run with a fly ball, two more with a home run, and another with a single. It was after that fifth game that he had all of his hits. There was a story that came out later, about Mr. Mack asking Earnshaw what Pepper was hitting. "Everything we throw," George said. He was just about right.

Late in the game, I think it was the seventh inning, Foxx hit a line drive that whacked me in the shin. Boy, I can tell you how hard he could hit a ball! Speaking from painful experience, you might say. The ball caromed off into right field and I felt for a moment like it had taken half my leg with it. I stood there on the mound with that foot lifted, not wanting to put it back down for fear it might be broken. It swelled up so fast that by the time I got back to the bench it looked like I had a baseball tucked into my stocking. But I finished up all right.

We went back to St. Louis on the train that night and Doc Weaver was putting ice packs on my leg to try and keep the swelling down. Pepper and some of the fellows were sitting around watching. Pepper was by this time a national hero. Judge Landis was making the trip with us and he came walking through the car. He stopped to ask me how I was and then somebody introduced Pepper to the Judge.

Pepper Martin. ". . . we had a secret weapon waiting for them."

"Well, Mr. Pepper Martin," the Judge said with a big grin, shaking hands with Pepper. "What I wouldn't give to be in your shoes."

Pepper looked at him and said, "I'd be happy to make the switch, Judge. I'd trade my sixty-five hundred a year for your sixty-five thousand any day."

We all laughed, the Judge the loudest.

The next day Lefty Grove came out firing bullets and they beat us 8–1. That made the Series three games apiece.

Burleigh Grimes started the seventh game for us against big George Earnshaw. We jumped off to a 4–0 lead by the third inning and Burleigh nursed it along until the top of the ninth. Then he got into some rough waters and gave up two runs and had men on first and second with two out. Burleigh had been having some trouble with his side, a pulled muscle or something, and he decided he had better come out right then and there. You can be sure he must have been in great pain, because he was a tough customer, that Grimes, and he hated to come out of a game.

So they brought me in to pitch. The batter was Max Bishop. Again, here was this fellow I didn't like to pitch to. I went to a full count with him and burned one in there. He lifted an easy fly ball to Pepper in center, and that's how the Series ended—the Pepper Martin Series—with a fly ball right into the glove of the man himself.

Well, as I said before, you just never know what's going to happen when you decide to try and make a career of baseball. You work your way up gradually, from the sandlots to semipro, then into the minor leagues, then finally up to the big leagues. That first spring training with the big team is unforgettable and so is the first regular season game you play in. Well, you say to yourself, nothing can top this. But then you have a good year and become a regular, maybe even a star. And then all of a sudden you've won a pennant and surely nothing can ever top that. But then there's the World Series, and that's got to be the topper of toppers. Just starting a World Series game is a thrill that's hard to describe. And when you're part of a championship ball club and maybe even did something important to help win it, well, then you're on the mountaintop and there's nowhere else to go.

Nowhere else? Well, of course there is. You can't stay up there forever and eventually you have to start making that trip in the other direction. I would often wonder how a fellow felt when he wasn't able to throw anymore. I used to watch some of the veteran pitchers who were losing their stuff and I would think: How does that feel? Well, you're bound to find out for yourself, aren't you? The realization sneaks up on you. All of a sudden it strikes you that your fast one is taking just a little longer to get there. Guys you never had trouble with before are getting out in front of it and pulling it.

No, you don't want to believe it at first. You tell yourself that if you get into better shape it will come back. Of course you're already in good shape. But little by little you start becoming realistic. There's no avoiding it. It's the toughest thing in the world to have to face up to, and not just because it was your bread and butter, but because it was something you took pride in. Fastball pitchers take an awful lot of pride in being able to zing that thing in there.

The only thing that makes it a little easier to take is the good memories. They start becoming more and more important. Somebody asked me just the other day if I had any regrets about having gone into baseball. Heavens no, I said. I think I made the right decisions when I was a young man. You know, there are always a lot of forks in the road and you're never sure which is the right one to take. I always trusted to judgment. No, I wouldn't want to do it all over again. I'm more than satisfied with the way things went. If I tried to do it over again, maybe it wouldn't pan out as well as it did.

Johnny Podres

JOHN JOSEPH PODRES

Born: September 30, 1932, Witherbee, New York
Major League career: 1953–1967, 1969, Brooklyn and Los Angeles Dodgers, Detroit Tigers, San Diego Padres
Lifetime record: 148 wins, 116 losses

Johnny Podres' most memorable moment on a ball field occurred in the seventh game of the 1955 World Series when, in shutting out the Yankees he pitched the Brooklyn Dodgers to their first, and only, World Series victory. That single game overshadows a long and productive big league career, during which Podres also won three other World Series games. In 1957 he led the National League in earned run average and shutouts, and in 1961 his 18–5 record gave him the league lead in winning percentage.

THERE MUST have been twenty-five or thirty cops around me. I was right in the middle of them, like the President of the United States. They were escorting me to the team bus for the ride back to Brooklyn. There was no way I could have walked out of Yankee Stadium by myself that day.

In baseball—well, I guess it's true of any sport—if your name becomes identified with one game or one event it'll stick forever. Hell, it's more than twenty years ago now, but I still meet a lot of people who when they hear my name start talking about that game. Of course it wasn't just winning a World Series, although you can't ever underestimate that; it was the fact that it was the Dodgers' first Series win ever. I knew a little bit about Dodger history—they had been in seven World Series since 1916 and had never won one. Sure, I knew that. You couldn't help but know it, the way the papers were playing it up in New York. But I don't think it was a factor one way or the other as far as I was concerned.

There was a hell of a party that night at the Hotel Bossert in Brooklyn. The champagne was really pouring. All you had to do was hold out your glass and somebody would fill it right up. The streets were filled with people and every so often I had to go out and wave to them, then go back inside again to the handshakes, the pats on the back, the champagne. Boy, the champagne! There was one guy there who kept telling me he'd been waiting for this since 1916. Can you imagine waiting thirty-nine years for something? I don't know how late that party went, or if it ever ended at all. The next morning a big limousine came by and picked me up and took me to the "Today" show. I must have still been feeling pretty good because I said, right out on the air, that I could beat the Yankees any day of the week. I was up so high I don't think I knew what I was saying. I didn't really come down until a few weeks later. I was at a deer camp in the Adirondacks, tramping through the woods by myself. It was a clear, crisp October day. All of a sudden I stopped and said to myself, "Hey, Podres, you beat the Yankees in the World Series!"

The next year, 1956, by rights should have been a great one for me. I was really riding a crest then. I had a tremendous amount of confidence and a certain amount of stature. I was only twenty-three years old at the time. I would ask myself: Where do you go from here, kiddo? Well, I'll tell you where I went: Into the United States Navy.

I still don't know how that happened. In 1952 I had been classified 4-F because of a back problem. Then all of a sudden I'm reclassified 1-A, and off I go. I'm not saying I shouldn't have gone in the Service; what I am saying is, why was I 4-F in 1952 and then all of a sudden 1-A in 1956? Was the World Series victory and all the publicity surrounding it a factor? It might have been. A lot of people probably said, "Here's this young, healthy guy, strong enough to win a World Series—why isn't he in the Service?" It might have created a public relations problem for somebody. I don't know.

Anyway, once I got into boot training my back didn't stand up under the gaff. They ended up putting me in a master-at-arms shack and got me a hospital bed to sleep on. I was living by myself. Then I

Johnny Podres

went to Norfolk, pitched a few innings, and in six months they let me out. I missed the whole season in 1956.

A year after I got out of the Service the team moved to Los Angeles. We won the pennant there in '59 and played the White Sox in the Series. I won the second game, with some help from Larry Sherry. I started the sixth game and should have won that one, too. Hell, I had an 8–0 lead going into the bottom of the fourth and was really breezing. Never felt better. But I'll tell you what was happening. Early Wynn started for the White Sox and he knocked down a few of our guys. Early was pretty good for coming in close to a guy. They started grumbling on the bench. "Knock somebody on their ass."

So in the bottom of the fourth I figured it was a good time. I had a man out, nobody on base and an 8–0 lead. Jim Landis was the batter. I wanted to brush him back a little bit. So I threw one. It was a good brush-back pitch, high and inside. The problem was, Landis had decided to bunt, and damn if he didn't go right into the ball. The thing sailed up and got him square in the head. If he had been standing up straight nothing would have happened. But he got hit and fell to the ground. When he went down I started shaking. You never want to hit anybody like that. It turned out he wasn't badly hurt, but I didn't know it at the time.

Hitting him like that shook me up so bad I lost my composure. I walked the next guy, fell behind to Ted Kluszewski and grooved one which he hit into the right-field stands. Then I walked the next guy. The next guy who walked was Walter Alston and the one after him was me. Larry Sherry came in and finished the game.

I won another game in the '63 Series, against the Yankees. Yeah, I had pretty good luck in the World Series, winning four and losing only one. But the one everybody always remembers is that seventh game against the Yankees in 1955, the one that gave the Dodgers their first championship, and the only one they ever won in Brooklyn.

You know, it doesn't always pan out that you sign with your favorite team, but that's what happened with me. I was always a Brooklyn fan. When I was a kid I used to stay up at night listening to Red Barber and Connie Desmond announcing the games. Their voices became so familiar to me it was like they were members of the family. Did I ever dream about winning the World Series for the Dodgers? Well, maybe. If you're a kid who wants to be a big league ball player those thoughts are going to slip in now and then. What do they call it—the impossible dream?

The guys who were going to be my teammates a few years later were already there. Pee Wee Reese, Jackie Robinson, Gil Hodges, Duke Snider, Carl Furillo, Roy Campanella, Billy Cox, Preacher Roe. Many a quiet night I'd sit in my room listening to Barber and Desmond telling me what those guys were doing in Brooklyn, or in St. Louis or Cincinnati or Pittsburgh, or wherever they were. The nights were always quiet where I lived. That was Witherbee, New York. In the Adirondacks. Beautiful country. Just beautiful. That's where I started playing ball, throwing them back and forth to my father when I was

Jackie Robinson stealing home in August, 1948, against the Boston Braves. The catcher is Bill Salkeld, the batter Billy Cox, the umpire Jocko Conlon.

six or seven years old. He was a semipro pitcher and I used to go and watch him pitch every Sunday. When I was old enough, I'd go out there in batting practice and shag balls, always making sure to put one or two in my pocket so I'd have a new ball to start the week off with.

There was one disadvantage growing up in the Adirondacks—the climate forced a short baseball season on you. Compared to the guys who grew up in, say, California or Florida, we barely had a chance to play. Our high school schedule was limited to ten or eleven games and sometimes a couple of those would be snowed out in the spring.

How did I get started in pro ball? Well, not many scouts come through Witherbee, New York. But I was lucky. My high school principal was a baseball fan and he took an interest in me. He knew a Dodger scout and got him to come up and have a look. The night the scout came up I pitched a no-hitter. He came back a second time to see me and I pitched another no-hitter. Then he invited me to come down to Brooklyn and work out at Ebbets Field with the Dodgers. This was in 1950. They signed me to a contract and I went away in 1951. I got a $6000 bonus. Actually $5200 was the bonus and $800 was my salary for 1951. Yeah, in 1951 I got paid $160 a month for five months.

They started me off at Newport News in the Piedmont League. I pitched there for a month and wasn't doing so hot and was sent down to Hazard, Kentucky in the Mountain States League. Class D ball. Screw up there and you're never heard from again. First game with Hazard I gave up seven runs in the first inning. I said to myself, "Boy, where do I go from here?" But then I got myself together and pitched shutout ball the rest of the way and won the game. I ended up that season with a 21–3 record.

When I came home after the season I needed a job. I went over to Republic Steel—they had an office in town—and asked them if they'd hire me, in the mines or on the surface. Witherbee was a mining town in those days. My father worked his whole life in the mines, taking out iron ore. I wasn't crazy about the idea of going into the mines, but hell, I needed a job. I kept pestering them and finally they gave me a job on the surface, in one of the mills. But if I hadn't been a ball player I eventually would have had to go into the mines, like most of my friends.

The next year I went to spring training with the Dodgers. I almost made the club, too. That would have been a hell of a jump, from Class D to the big leagues. But they sent me to Montreal instead. A year later, though, I made the club, even though I didn't have such a good spring. I had come in at the right time, you see, when the Dodgers really needed left-handed pitching. The only other lefty on the team that year was Preacher Roe.

I joined the Dodgers a year or so ahead of Koufax. He was just a wild, hard-throwing left-hander then. It took him about five years, but he finally turned it around. I think the Dodgers were getting ready to give up on him, but then overnight he put it all together and for the next five or six years was the best pitcher I saw. He became a perfectionist out there. Hell, he got to the point where he'd get mad at himself for walking a guy. It was hard to believe this was the same pitcher who a few years before couldn't find the plate.

I would say that for the years I was watching him, Koufax was tops. But for the long haul, for year-after-year performance, Warren Spahn was the best I ever saw. He was just a master of his trade. When he was out there I couldn't take my eyes off him. I'd watch him work on the good hitters—he was always pitching them from behind so they would be swinging at the pitch *he* wanted them to hit. Great control. Watching him was an education. You know, the guy pitched over twenty years and hardly ever missed a turn. I don't think he knew what a sort arm was. And another thing about Spahn: He didn't win his first game in the big leagues until he was twenty-five years old, and he still ended up with 363 lifetime wins.

Robin Roberts was another great one. He pitched ball games just as good as he had to. I used to watch him time after time get into a jam, bases loaded and nobody out or something like that. You'd get the feeling on the bench: Okay, we got him now. One more hit will do it. But, damn, that hit wouldn't come. All of a sudden the guy is

Warren Spahn in 1942. "He was just a master of his trade."

reaching back and firing harder and harder. Next thing you knew there were two strikeouts and a ground ball and you were wondering where the hell your rally went. Roberts always had it when he needed it.

But talk about talent, those Dodger teams in the 1950's had it. Pee Wee Reese, Jackie Robinson, Roy Campanella, Jim Gilliam, Carl Furillo, Gil Hodges, Duke Snider. For pitchers we had Don Newcombe, Carl Erskine, Clem Labine.

One of the problems with a club like that, with so many outstanding players, the sportswriters couldn't give each guy the coverage he deserved. When a team has two or three good players, then those guys get all the attention and the publicity. But with the team we had, with a couple of guys doing something spectacular every day with the bat or the glove, who were you going to focus on?

I'll tell you, it made me a much better pitcher, playing with those guys. And I don't mean just because they got me the runs and made the plays. It was just that being surrounded by so much talent made you work harder and play harder. There was no other way, if you wanted to stay on the same field with them.

Even when we lost the first two games to the Yankees in the '55 Series those guys were still confident they were going to win. We figured once we got them in Ebbets Field we'd knock them around a little.

I had no idea I'd be starting in the Series. We had Newcombe, Erskine, Roger Craig, Billy Loes, Karl Spooner. I honestly didn't think I'd get a start. You see, I really didn't have an outstanding year in '55. I started off okay, winning seven of my first ten, but then hurt my shoulder. I was on the disabled list for a while and when I came back it took me some time to get squared away.

Then when I was okay again and getting back into the groove, I had a freak accident in September, at Ebbets Field. Batting practice was over and we were getting set to take infield. I had a fungo bat and was going to hit fly balls to the outfielders. Well, in Ebbets Field they used to wheel the batting cage across the diamond and out through a gate in center field. They started wheeling that thing and, jeez, they hit me right in the side with it. Banged up my ribs pretty good. For two or three weeks I could hardly breathe. It was so bad they were thinking of bringing somebody up from Montreal and putting me back on the disabled list, which would have kept me out of the Series.

But then after we'd cinched the pennant I pitched a game against the Pirates. This was about a week or so before the Series. I pitched four innings and had real good stuff, so they decided I was okay. If I hadn't looked all right in that game I don't think I would have pitched in the Series; I would have gone on the disabled list. Sometimes when I think of how close I came to not playing in the '55 Series I break out in a cold sweat.

Roy Campanella

Newcombe and Loes started the first two games at Yankee Stadium and we got beat. After the second game Alston told me to be ready tomorrow, that I was opening in Ebbets Field. I felt just great about it. The fact that he was picking me when we had our backs to the wall was a real compliment. It showed the confidence he had in me.

I beat the Yankees that third game, 8–3. Campanella got us going in the first inning with a home run off of Bob Turley, and we kept going. That game got us turned around. We won the next two and the

Series went back to Yankee Stadium. We needed just one more to wrap it up. But Whitey Ford stopped us, 5–1.

We were all pretty blue after that game. I remember Reese was sitting in front of his locker with his head down and I said to him, "Don't worry, Pee Wee. I'll shut 'em out tomorrow." You've got to say something, what the hell.

Alston had told me before the sixth game, "You're the pitcher tomorrow if we don't win it today." So I knew. After we lost the sixth game, then I knew for sure. Well, I told myself, one more day's work to do. I went home that night and didn't think too much about it. I don't believe I ever in my life thought about a game I was going to pitch the next day. Why worry today about what you've got to do tomorrow?

I woke up that morning and had the same breakfast I'd had the day I pitched the third game. At the same time, too. Superstitious? No. Careful.

When I got out to the ball park, that's when I started getting keyed up. It wasn't just the seventh game either, it was walking into the ball park. That always keyed me up. Still does. That's when my clock starts to tick.

I remember I warmed up with Dixie Howell, who was our third-string catcher. When they announced the Yankee lineup I said to him, "Dixie, there's no way that lineup can beat me today." I guess I was trying to give myself a little boost.

One break I got was Mickey Mantle didn't play that day. He was injured. But so was Jackie Robinson. Neither one started.

You know, in the game I beat them 8–3 I threw a lot of change-ups. I had that pitch working just right and it really helped me. I think they were looking for it in the seventh game. I did throw some in the first three or four innings and again it was effective, but over the last five I stayed pretty much with the fastball. If you've got it, that's a good pitch to throw in Yankee Stadium that time of year, with the ball flashing from sunlight into shadow. No, we didn't deliberately change the pattern. Campy saw how well my hard stuff was working and he told me to stay with it, especially when those shadows started growing longer.

In the last of the eighth the Yankees had men on first and third and two out and I fanned Hank Bauer on as good a fastball as I ever threw in my life. I started it around his letters and when he swung and missed the ball was up at his shoulders.

But of course the play that everybody remembers in that Series is Sandy Amoros' catch. You can't talk about the '55 Series with anybody for more than a minute before they start talking about that play.

We were leading 2–0 in the bottom of the sixth and the Yankees got their first two batters on first and second. Gil McDougald on second, Billy Martin on first. Berra's the batter. He was a left-handed hitter and we played him to pull. He was a dead pull hitter. But the son of a gun lifted a ball out to left field. At first I wasn't worrying about it. In fact, when he hit it I bent over and picked up the rosin bag and said to myself, "Well, there's one out." But then I looked around and saw the ball keep slicing toward the line and I saw Amoros running his tail off. "Jeez," I said to myself, "he's got a hell of a run." The ball seemed to hang up in the air forever, and Amoros is *still* running. I started to think: *Is he going to get it?* I'll tell you, that's a helpless goddamned feeling, standing on the mound at a moment like that. The game was close, the tying runs are on base, all the marbles have gone up in the air on that ball, and there's your out-fielder running for it and all of a sudden I started getting this sickly feeling that maybe he *wasn't* going to be there when the ball came down.

But he was, and, jeez, just barely. At the last moment, still going at top speed, he reached out and that baby dropped right into his glove. I let out a sigh—I guess I'd been holding my breath.

Martin, who was on second, hadn't gone off too far; but McDougald, who was on first, must have thought the ball was going to drop in. He had to be thinking that, because he was just about going around second base when Amoros made the catch, and he had to put the brakes on. We had McDougald hung out to dry and all we needed was a couple of good throws to get him. I remember Reese going out to take the cut-off. Just before he got the ball from Amoros, Pee Wee took a quick look around to see where the runners were, and then

Amoros hit him with a perfect peg. As soon as Pee Wee got the ball he didn't hesitate a second—he knew where he had to send it.

I'm still standing there on the mound—all this is happening in a matter of seconds—watching it the same as everybody else. Pee Wee whips around and fires that ball to Hodges at first base. There's McDougald trying to get back. Pee Wee made a perfect throw and we had McDougald nailed from here to Christmas.

Boy, did that juice me up. I got the next guy out, got them out in the seventh and eighth, then nailed the first two men in the ninth. One more to go. I was so hepped up I could hardly stand still out there. I just *knew* I was going to get that last batter and couldn't wait. It was Elston Howard. I wanted to finish up with a strikeout and I threw him fastball after fastball—good, hard, riding fastballs— but he kept fouling them off. Campanella called for another fastball but I shook him off. I think it was the only time in the whole game I did that. I threw a change-up and Howard hit it down to Reese at short. When Pee Wee saw the ball coming at him a big grin broke

Sandy Amoros. "I started to think: *Is he going to get it?*"

across his face; I guess he couldn't help it. He made a low throw to first but Hodges picked it up without any trouble.

A lot of what happened after that is a blur. I wish I could remember it all, because I'm sure I had a hell of a good time.

Phil Cavaretta

Phil Cavaretta

PHILIP JOSEPH CAVARETTA

Born: July 19, 1916, Chicago, Illinois
Major League career: 1934–1955, Chicago Cubs, Chicago White Sox
Lifetime record: .293

One of the most durable players in baseball history, Phil Cavaretta played in the big leagues for twenty-two years, and always in a Chicago uniform —twenty years with the Cubs and two with the White Sox. Cavaretta's greatest year was 1945 when he led the National League in batting with a .355 average. The year before, he led the league with 197 hits. Cavaretta played in three World Series and in two of them posted batting averages of .462 and .423.

I THINK if you ask any major leaguer, he'll tell you that he started playing ball almost as soon as he could walk and that it was always his ambition to play in the big leagues. I know it was that way with players from my era. I used to be out there every day, knocking the ball around with my friends. If you like to play baseball you'll always have a lot of friends. We used to stay at it until dark, until we could no longer see the ball. Many was the time I walked into the house and found my father waiting for me. He was from Italy and he didn't understand baseball.

"Where've you been?" he would ask.

"Out playing a little baseball."

"Baseball?" he would say, giving me this very quizzical look. "You don't play baseball—you go to school and get an education."

He was right about that, of course. You should get an education, and I probably would have, except that things happened so fast. I was hoping for a crack at professional baseball, just to see how good I was.

217

I signed with the Cubs in '34 and started the season with Peoria in the Central League, went on to Reading in the New York–Pennsylvania League and then finished out the season with the Cubs. All in the matter of a few months. Talk about going up the ladder in a hurry! Why, just the year before I was one of the kids waiting outside the gate to watch them come out after the game. I never bothered them for autographs; I was interested in them as people. I just wanted to see their faces close up, see the way they walked, the way they dressed. You know, get a feeling of them as *human beings.* I liked Gabby Hartnett a lot, and Billy Herman was one of my favorites. And then—hard to believe—a year later those men were my teammates, and a year and a half later I was rooming with Billy Herman. I got into seven games at the end of the '34 season and hit .381.

Once you've had a taste of the big leagues, you want to stay there, believe me. That's all I had on my mind that winter—sticking with the Cubs. They had always been my team anyway. I was born and raised on the near North Side, which was Cub country. Playing in the big leagues was great in itself, but playing with the Cubs, well, that was the icing on the cake.

In 1935 I went to spring training with the ball club, did okay and became the regular first baseman. I've always felt that was one of the best Cub teams ever. It was a mix of young fellows like myself, Billy Herman, Stan Hack, Billy Jurges, Augie Galan, Frank Demaree, and veterans like Gabby Hartnett, Chuck Klein, Fred Lindstrom. We had strong pitching, too, with Lon Warneke, Bill Lee, Larry French, Charlie Root, Roy Hensaw, Tex Carleton.

Most of the season it was a fight between the Giants and the Cardinals. We were watching them from third place. But then in September we put on a real drive. We won twenty-one straight games. You ever go seventy-five miles an hour on the highway while everybody else is doing fifty? That's how we felt. We passed the Giants and caught up to the Cardinals right at the end of the season.

With everything up for grabs, we went into St. Louis for a five-game series. All we needed was to win two of the five. At that time the streak had grown to eighteen in a row. In the first game Lon

Left to right, Larry French, Charlie Grimm, and Freddie Lindstrom in California, spring of 1935

Warneke beat Paul Dean 1–0. It was no score going into the eighth inning and I hit a home run. I didn't hit many home runs as a rule, but that was a good one. I traveled around those bases feeling like Babe Ruth. The next day Bill Lee, who was one fine pitcher, beat Dizzy. That clinched the pennant for us, but we won the next game too, just for luck. They finally beat us to stop the streak, but by then it didn't matter.

I'll always remember that win streak. As we were piling it up day by day it didn't seem like such an unusual thing, but looking back on it now I can see it was quite an achievement. It just caught on and kept building. We got the breaks and we made the breaks. In a streak like that everything has got to go your way, your line drives have to get through, your bloopers have to fall, your hit-and-runs have to work, your pitchers have to be right. It's got to be a good, hard team effort, and that's just what that streak was. When you're able to put together a twenty-one-game winning streak you know you have a *team*.

So in my first full year in the big leagues, at the age of nineteen, I got to play in a World Series, against the Detroit Tigers. Sure I was nervous. I know that in the first game things didn't go too well for me. I didn't get the ball out of the infield. But we won anyway. Lon Warneke shut the Tigers out 3–0. And that was no easy thing to do against that ball club. The Tigers had a powerful lineup, with fellows like Mickey Cochrane, Hank Greenberg, Goose Goslin, Charlie Gehringer, Pete Fox. They're all in the Hall of Fame today, with the exception of Fox.

After the game, some of my teammates kind of took me in hand and got me to relax. I remember Billy Herman talking to me, and Augie Galan, Larry French, and Charlie Grimm, who was the manager.

Still, it was a rough Series for me. I didn't get a hit through my first thirteen at bats, until the fourth game. It's true I was a little nervous, but maybe that Detroit pitching had something to do with it—Schoolboy Rowe, Tommy Bridges, Alvin Crowder, Eldon Auker. That was quite a staff to have bearing down against you in a short series.

The Series went six games and Detroit beat us. The last game was a tough one for us. The score was tied 3–3 when we came to bat in the top of the ninth inning. Stanley Hack led off against Tommy Bridges with a triple. He just blasted that thing out to center field. So there's the leading run on third base with nobody out. But we never got him home. Billy Jurges was the next batter and he struck out. Then Larry French, the pitcher, came up. He bounced back to Bridges. Augie Galan made the third out, on a fly ball that came too late.

Now, there's been some controversy down through the years about that. Charlie Grimm has been second-guessed up and down the line for letting French hit in that spot. But I'll tell you something I don't think many people know about. We had been having trouble with the plate umpire, George Moriarity. Some close decisions had gone against us and there was a lot of heat coming from our dugout. Finally in around the sixth or seventh inning, Moriarity threw quite a few of our players out of the game. That included some guys who Grimm could have used to pinch-hit. So when that situation cropped up in the ninth he just didn't have anybody available. I would imagine he would have used a batter for Jurges as well as for French, if he'd had them. But unfortunately we had nobody there.

In the bottom of the ninth the Tigers won it. It was the first world championship ever for Detroit. With all the great players they had had through the years, like Cobb, Harry Heilmann, and all the rest, they had never won a World Series. Just a year before, the Cardinals had beaten them in seven games. So that pump was primed. Those fans were on the edges of their seats, waiting for it.

Earl Averill, Jimmie Foxx, Lou Gehrig, Goose Goslin, and Pinky Higgins at the 1936 All-Star game

With one out Mickey Cochrane got a hit. Charlie Gehringer came up and, boy, did he hit a shot right at me! It was one of those instances when you see a man swing a bat and a split second later there's a line drive exploding right on top of you. I played in the big leagues for another twenty years and I can't remember too many balls that were ever hit harder at me on first base. More in self-protection than anything else, I threw up my gloved hand. The ball tore right on through and I was just about able to stop it with my bare hand. If I had knocked it down with my glove I could have gone to second with it and forced Cochrane. But the ball had really stung my bare hand and I was in so much pain that I didn't want to risk a throw to second. I was afraid it might wind up in left field. So I took the sure way out and stepped on first. But that got Cochrane to second.

Goose Goslin was the next batter. He was a tough old veteran, a great hitter. French jammed him with an inside pitch and Goslin got just enough bat on it to loop it over the head of my old roomie Billy Herman into right field. The ball fell in. It was picked up in the out-field—by either Frank Demaree or Chuck Klein—and I moved in as the cut-off man. There's always been some debate about my cutting off the relay home. Well, Cochrane was crossing home plate before the ball even reached me. I took one look at that and cut the ball off. A lot of people thought I should have let it go through, but the game was already over. Remember, it was two out and Cochrane was running the moment the ball was hit. But people like to have something to talk about, don't they? I think a lot of it came from disappointment, as if to say, "If only the throw were allowed to go through we might have got him." No way. They could have shot it in from the outfield with a rifle and still no way.

But you can't imagine how frustrating it was to see that ball bloop up into the air and know it wasn't going to be caught. There's the World Series sitting on that thing, and here it's dropping real soft and harmless right down on the grass with Herman a few steps short and Demaree a few steps short and Klein a few steps short. They say it's a game of seconds and inches, and it's very true; and that's why I think that sometimes the disappointment stays with the loser longer than the elation stays with the winner.

Since I was part of the group, it may be immodest of me to say so, but I still feel that the infield we had on the Cubs in '35 was the best ever in Chicago. Yes sir, better even than the Tinker to Evers to Chance infields. I wouldn't say it if I didn't honestly believe it. Billy Herman, Billy Jurges, Stan Hack—those guys were all good, smart ball players. As a matter of fact, the four of us eventually managed in the big leagues.

In '38, when we won the pennant again, Rip Collins was on the club and he played first base and I went to the outfield. Otherwise there weren't too many changes from the '35 team.

That was the year we switched managers in midseason. Charlie Grimm went out and Gabby Hartnett came in. It's unusual to have a managerial switch in the middle of the season and still win the pennant. I know it happened to the Cubs before, in 1932, when Rogers Hornsby was let out and Grimm took over. I wasn't with the team then but I remember that. Charlie was a good manager and an easygoing sort of person. Possibly we needed a little more discipline on the club. I think this is probably the main reason they made the change—they couldn't have been too unhappy with Charlie since they brought him back to manage again in the 1940's for about six years.

Gabby was a good-natured guy but he could be very stern when he had to. He saw that the discipline was imposed and the team really came to life after that. We started to jell.

We went at it with Pittsburgh that year and it was Gabby who hit that famous home run against them near the end of the season. They call it "The home run in the dark," which is just about what it was. I guess it's one of the most famous home runs ever hit.

The Pirates came into Wrigley Field for a three-game series leading us by a game-and-a-half. Dizzy Dean pitched the opener for us and he beat them a close game. Now we're only a half-game out.

The next day we went into the bottom of the ninth tied at 5–5. It had been a long afternoon and now it was starting to get dark. As everybody knows, Wrigley Field has no lights, so this was going to be the last time at bat for anybody. No question but that the game was going to be called. Mace Brown was pitching for the Pirates. He

Gabby Hartnett, left, and Dizzy Dean in 1938

was a great relief pitcher. I'd say just about the best in the league at that time.

Brown retired the first two men and then got two strikes over on Gabby, fastballs that he just fired right through there. Then for some reason he decided he was going to throw a slider. Why he wanted to do that I can't understand; the fastball would have made more sense in that light. But that's what he threw and Gabby hit a line drive into the left-field bleachers. But fastball or slider, to this day I don't know how Hartnett ever saw that ball, much less was able to hit it out.

That home run left the Pirates in a state of shock. They were still only a half-game behind us, but we ran over them by a big score the next day and went on to win it.

In '38 we played the Yankees in the World Series. They were steamrollers in those years. When you talk about great ball clubs you can't overlook the 1938 Yankees. Lou Gehrig, Joe DiMaggio, Bill Dickey, Joe Gordon, Red Rolfe, Tommy Henrich. And along with all of that hitting they had Red Ruffing, Lefty Gomez, Johnny Murphy, and that side-armer, Monte Pearson.

What can you say when you're wiped out in four straight? Of course when you sit down later and take inventory you realize what a great ball club you were up against and that takes some of the sting out of it. But still. I had a pretty good Series personally, hitting .462, but there's not much satisfaction in that if you don't win. It's like hitting a home run when your team is ten runs down. It's nice, but so what?

Nevertheless, I have some pleasant memories from that World Series. In one game, I believe it was the third, I got on first with a base hit. Gehrig came over to hold me on.

"Young man," he said, "I like the way you play. If you continue to play that way you'll be in the big leagues a long time."

Well, you can imagine how I felt. You don't forget those things, especially coming from somebody like Lou Gehrig.

Standing close to him, you wouldn't have thought there was anything wrong with Gehrig. He looked strong, in very good health. But he did seem kind of sluggish in the field. I don't think he ran too well and there was something missing in the way he swung the bat. That illness had already begun to affect him. He had to retire the next spring. Another two years and he was dead. I'll never forget him. He was one fine gentleman.

Probably the most memorable thing in that Series was the way Dizzy Dean pitched for us. We had bought Diz from the Cardinals that spring. His arm was just about shot, but still he won a few games for us. He was pitching on heart and know-how more than anything else. He knew how to pitch, too. Dizzy Dean wasn't just a thrower, not even when he had his great stuff. I don't think it's widely appreciated just how knowledgeable and shrewd a pitcher he always was on that mound. That's why he was so great in his prime. He not only could bring it up there in a hurry—we called him "The Express"— but he knew the batters and he had control. To me his fastball was

Wes Ferrell, left, and Lefty Gomez, opening day pitchers at Yankee Stadium in 1936

almost like a breaking ball, it had so much on it. He threw it high and it would rise on you. It was always moving.

Dean started the second game of the Series, at Wrigley Field. You had to watch him pitch-by-pitch to appreciate what he was doing. Slow curves, good control, and occasionally he'd reach back and zip one through there. For heart and courage, it was the greatest game I ever saw pitched. Remember, he was up against an extremely hard-hitting lineup and for seven innings he had them beat, 3–2. We got some runs off of Lefty Gomez early in the game and Diz nursed them along. But then in the eighth inning Frank Crosetti hit a two-run homer and in the ninth DiMaggio did the same thing. We lost the game 6–3. But for seven innings he handled them just fine, giving up only two or three hits.

When it was over we patted him on the back and told him what a good job he'd done. He just smiled. He was philosophical about things. I never heard him complain about his arm injury, what it cost him. He was only around twenty-six when it happened. It just about stopped his career at midpoint and there's no telling what records he might have put in the book if it hadn't happened.

Diz was a great guy. And a prankster. I'm sure everybody knows that. He would get a dollar bill and tape a piece of white string to it and then go and sit down in the hotel lobby with the string in his hand and the dollar bill out in the middle of the floor. Somebody would come along, see the dollar and bend over for it and Diz would snap it away from them. Or sometimes he would start moving it slowly toward him and you'd be surprised, some people kept moving after it, crouched over with their hands reaching out, so intent on picking up that money that it never occurred to them to wonder why a dollar bill should be sliding on the floor.

I had my best year in 1945. I had lots of good fortune all season and ended up leading the league with .355. It was a tight pennant race, too. The Cardinals had won three in a row and everybody figured them to run away with it. But we stayed with them all year and beat them out by a few games. We played Detroit in the Series that October. Same team the Cubs had played ten years before. I think the only players who participated in both of those Series were myself and Stan Hack with the Cubs and Hank Greenberg with Detroit. That was the year the war ended and Hank had come out of the Service in the middle of the season to help Detroit win it.

You did the best you could during the war years. A lot of ball players had been drafted and the teams were a mix of young and old, experience and inexperience. But still, I maintain we had a pretty good ball club in Chicago in 1945. Along with Hack and myself, we had Bill Nicholson, Andy Pafko, Peanuts Lowery, and some good pitchers like Hank Borowy, Paul Derringer, Claude Passeau, Hank Wyse.

It turned out to be a good Series—seven games. But unfortunately we lost. I still to this day feel we had the better team. They won the seventh game on the strength of a big first inning. Hank Borowy had already pitched three times for us when he started the seventh game

Paul Derringer in 1939

and he just ran out of gas. The Tigers scored two runs and had the bases loaded. Paul Richards came up and unloaded them with a double. Boy, was that a crusher. Paul was never noted for his hitting, but he hit one that time. I'll bet that's the biggest hit he ever got in his life. We just weren't able to come back from it.

I had a good Series—eleven hits and a .423 average, but I was still disappointed. That was my third Series and I really wanted to be on a winner. But I shouldn't complain. At least I had my shots at it.

JOSEPH WHEELER SEWELL
CLEVELAND A. L., NEW YORK A. L.,
1920 – 1933
POSTED LIFETIME .312 BATTING AVERAGE,
TOPPING .300 IN TEN OF 14 YEARS. MOST
DIFFICULT MAN TO STRIKE OUT IN GAME'S
HISTORY. CREATED RECORDS WITH: FEWEST
CAREER STRIKEOUTS (114), FOUR SEASONS
OF FOUR WHIFFS OR LESS IN 500 AT-BATS
AND 115 GAMES IN ROW WITHOUT FANNING.
LED A.L. SHORTSTOPS IN FIELDING TWICE
AND IN PUTOUTS AND ASSISTS FOUR TIMES.

Joe Sewell Hall of Fame plaque

Joe Sewell

I GREW up in Titus, Alabama. That was a little town, way out in the country. Fifteen miles from the railroad. There wasn't too much going on around there, so baseball, which was an early interest for me and my brother Luke, kept getting more and more important in our lives as we grew up.

Oh yes, I followed the big leagues. Ty Cobb was my idol. Not only was he a great player, but he was from Georgia, you see, and since I was from Alabama, I felt sort of a kinship with him. When I got to the big leagues in 1920 Cobb was still playing. We played in the American League together for eight years and I'll tell you, every time I got out on the same field with him it was a tremendous thrill for me.

I got to be very friendly with Cobb. He was one of the finest men I ever met. I know that a lot of people didn't like him, but that was because of the way he played ball. When he put on that uniform he was a different person. It became a blood war and he was determined to beat the fire out of you. But away from the field I found him to be as nice a person as I ever sat down with. Highly intelligent. Loved to talk.

He was the greatest ball player that I ever saw. The records bear it out; but there were a lot of things he could do to beat you that don't show up in the records. He was always outsmarting you, adapting to a situation, on the go before you knew what was happening. If you gave him the slightest opening he would spy it and take advantage. Now, Ruth was a great ball player, but Cobb could do more things out there than Babe. I'll say this though: For accuracy, Ruth was the greatest throwing outfielder that I ever played with. When there was a man on first and the ball was hit to right field I just went over and put the bag between my feet. That ball would come out of

231

right field on one hop, smack into my glove. He seldom made a bad throw, maybe twice in the years I played on his side. For accuracy nobody could top him, not Speaker, not anybody.

To me it was very gratifying to think that I had enough ability to play with those fellows like Cobb and Ruth and Tris Speaker and Eddie Collins and Walter Johnson. Sometimes it's hard to believe what's happening to you. For years I read about Tris Speaker, about what a great all-around player he was, nearly the equal of Cobb. And then here I am one day joining the ball club where he's managing and playing center field, and he's calling me by my first name and treating me as an equal. I wish every boy who had the burning interest in baseball and the deep desire to play as I had, could have the chance to play in the major leagues.

Sure there was a lot of interest in Titus around World Series time. But what made it kind of frustrating for us boys was the fact that the scores didn't reach us until a day later. That's when we got the big city papers, from Birmingham or Montgomery. We would get yesterday's papers today. That was how we kept up with it.

One World Series I can still remember getting excited about was in 1914. That was the year the Boston Braves came from way behind to win the pennant and then upset Connie Mack's Athletics in four straight games. Our papers were full of that. George Stallings was the manager of the Braves and he had those three mighty fine pitchers who seemed to do all of the winning for his team—Dick Rudolph, Lefty Tyler, and Bill James. That team stands out in my memory because what they did was quite a feat. Mr. Mack had just a fine, fine team, with his own good pitchers like Chief Bender, Eddie Plank, Bullet Joe Bush. Nobody—nobody in Titus, Alabama, anyway— believed that anybody could beat the Athletics that year, much less in four straight. We pondered that one for a long time.

I might have lived my whole life in Titus without anybody ever hearing about me, if not for baseball. But I was lucky. I'm sure there were any number of boys who would have had fine careers if they had just been given the opportunity. You see, back in those days it was very easy for even an outstanding young player to be overlooked.

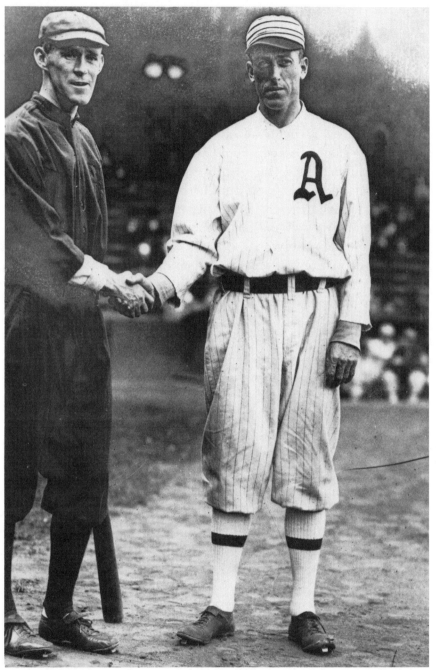

Johnny Evers, left, and Eddie Plank at the 1914 World Series

Today the big league clubs have scouts all over the country, plus a lot of other ways of conveying information about talented young players. It's unlikely that a boy would be overlooked today. But you couldn't say that when I was growing up, during those years after the turn of the century.

My father was a country doctor and he'd been to college. So he had seen the value of an education. There were six of us in the family and he was determined that each of us should have an education so as to be able to get the most out of whatever abilities we had. The school we attended was the University of Alabama. That's where we went, Luke and myself and our two brothers, while our sisters went to college in Montgomery.

I was supposed to be a doctor, like my father. In fact, I took pre-med; I was all set to study medicine. But at the same time I played baseball at the university. That was the ironic thing. The university had a highly developed and well-organized athletic program and it was through the exposure I got there that I landed with an industrial team in Birmingham. I played in the TCI League—that's the Tennessee Coal and Iron Company in Birmingham, a subsidiary of U.S. Steel. Each team represented a different town, like Tarrant City, Fairfield, Bessemer, and so on. It was a good brand of ball. Fellows went from that league up to the big leagues. I started there, so did my brother Luke, and so did Riggs Stephenson, one of the best hitters that ever lived.

It was playing in the TCI League that got me a contract with the New Orleans ball club, and they had an affiliation with the Cleveland Indians. Sure I was delighted when New Orleans offered me the contract. I never had any thought but to sign it. Was my father disappointed? No, he went along with it. You see, it was still my intention to study medicine, to go back to school after the season. But how could I have foreseen all the things that were going to happen to me over the next few months? I never did go back to school.

I came to the big leagues under the most tragic circumstances possible—to fill the job of a man who had died after being hit in the head by a pitched ball. To make it even more difficult for me, I had only about two months of professional experience under my belt, and to make it still more difficult, I was joining the ball club right in the middle of a red-hot pennant race.

I was in New Orleans when it happened. It was around the sixteenth or seventeenth of August, in 1920. I went downstairs to the hotel lobby in the morning and heard that the Cleveland shortstop, Ray Chapman, had died from the effects of being hit by a pitched ball thrown by Carl Mays of the Yankees. It never dawned on me that I was the next man in line for that job. What the heck, I was still pretty green. But then I was called into the office by the New Orleans manager, Johnny Dodds.

"How would you like to go to the big leagues?" he asked me.

I was a bit taken aback.

"I don't know," I said. I had never even seen a major league game, so I wasn't too sure.

Luke Sewell. "A tremendous asset to a ball club."

Joe Sewell in the early 1920s

"Well," he said, "the Cleveland Indians need a shortstop and you're the man they want."

"You reckon I can do the job?" I asked.

"You can play up there," he said. He seemed very positive about it. "In any event, you're leaving tonight. There's an eight o'clock train."

I played the ball game that afternoon, hit a double and a triple, and then hurried back to the hotel and got ready. I stepped aboard the train at eight o'clock still a little uncertain and bewildered—it was all happening so quickly. It took me that night and all the next day. I spent the night in Cincinnati, then caught the train the next morning and got into Cleveland in the middle of the afternoon. Excited? I'll say. Too excited even to talk. I don't think I said two words to anybody all the way to Cleveland.

But I'll tell you what happened. Remember now, I was coming out of New Orleans where it was real hot. When I got to Cincinnati, all I was wearing was a seersucker suit and a little sailor straw hat. Well, it was chilly up there—by my standards, anyway. I missed my train connection in Cincinnati and had to spend the night there. I checked into a little old hotel. I happened to mention to the desk clerk where I was going and that I needed heavier clothing.

"The stores are all closed," he said. It was after dark now. "But a friend of mine is a haberdasher. Let's see what we can drum up."

He called his friend and that fellow came down and opened his store and sold me a suit of clothes and a felt hat. While he was measuring me up, the haberdasher asked me why I was going to Cleveland. You know, just to make conversation.

"On business," I said.

I didn't tell him I was going up to the big leagues. I didn't think he would believe me. Heck, I still couldn't believe it myself.

Well, I finally got there, smack into a three-way pennant race between Cleveland, the Yankees, and the White Sox.

I never will forget the first game I saw. I wasn't in the lineup that day. I spent the whole afternoon on the bench. First of all, I almost fell off my feet when I saw that ball park—League Park. Biggest thing I ever saw in my life. Looked to me like they could get the whole city of Cleveland in there, if they wanted.

They were playing the Philadelphia Athletics. Everything that happened that day is as clear in my mind as if it happened yesterday. Doc Johnston was playing first base for the Indians and he got five base hits for five times up, and in one inning he stole home. Elmer Smith of the Indians went after a ball in right-center and at the last second jumped up against the fence and caught that ball backhanded. Just took a high line drive right off of the fence. My goodness, I thought, what a great catch. I figured I had got to the big leagues just in time to see one of the most wonderful plays ever made. But then Tris Speaker made two catches in center field that were just as good, if not better. Tilly Walker, who was playing center field for the Athletics, threw a man out at home plate with a peg that looked to me like it was a half mile long. All through that game I just kept slumping down further and further in the corner of the dugout, telling myself, "I don't think you belong here, Joe." They'd take one look at me and send me right back. And what was I going to do with that heavy suit of clothes in New Orleans?

The next day Speaker put me out at short in infield practice. He got one of the coaches, Jack McAllister, to hit balls to me. Well, he couldn't get one by me. I was all over the place, going into the hole and crossing second base, just picking up everything. Then I took some batting practice and I hit the ball very well. When I went back into the clubhouse, Speaker collared me and said, "Joe, you're playing shortstop today."

"Are you sure?" I asked. I didn't know what to say.

"Yes," he said. "Aren't you?"

"I guess I am," he said.

He smiled at me and patted me on the shoulder. I think he understood that I was a little nervous.

First time at bat I hit a line drive that Tilly Walker caught in center field. Then I came up again. Fellow named Scott Perry was out on the mound. He wound up and threw it. I never will forget that pitch. A high curve ball on the outside. I reached out and hit it right over the third baseman's head for a triple. I dropped my bat and just flew around those bases. When I got to third I stood there and said to myself, "Shucks, this ain't so tough after all." And I haven't been nervous from that day to this.

That was the year, if you recall, that the White Sox scandal came to light. They had thrown the World Series the year before but it wasn't until September of 1920 that the story broke. It happened right after we played them a series in Cleveland. The whole bunch of them, Joe Jackson, Eddie Cicotte and all the others, were suspended. With two weeks of the season still remaining they were declared ineligible and that put the White Sox out of the running. But the Yankees were still there. When it came down to it though, we beat them out.

We played Brooklyn in the World Series. They were called the Robins then, because of their manager, Wilbert Robinson. The Brooklyn Robins.

Brooklyn had a good team. But so did we. We had some outstanding players. I'm thinking of Tris Speaker and Elmer Smith and Charlie Jamieson and Larry Gardner. We had some very fine pitchers, too. Jim Bagby won thirty-one games that year, Stanley Coveleski won twenty-four, Ray Caldwell won twenty. That's seventy-five wins right there, from three pitchers. You get that, you don't need much more.

Coveleski pitched the first game in Brooklyn and beat Rube Marquard by a score of 3–1. I didn't get many hits in that Series but, I got one in the second inning that helped along a two-run rally, which was all Stanley really needed. But he had to pitch a close ball game because Marquard was a very tough pitcher, tough to hit. He had everything.

Burleigh Grimes shut us out the next day, 3–0. Burleigh was another good one. He had a live fastball and that spitball, the famous Burleigh Grimes spitball that was so hard to hit. We lost the third game too, 2–1, to Sherry Smith. Then the Series moved to Cleveland.

In the fourth game Stanley came back to beat them again, 5–1. Stanley was tough through the whole Series. But he was always tough. He was just a great pitcher, that's all.

Then came the fifth game. That's the famous one. One of the most historic games of baseball ever played. You just can't talk about World Series history without bringing up that game. As a matter of fact, I

Stanley Coveleski

was on the scene for *two* of the most historic games ever played, and I'll tell you about the other one later. But this fifth one in 1920, just looking at the score doesn't tell you much. It was 8–1, a very easy win for us. So you've got to look twice to get the story.

To start off, Elmer Smith made history in the first inning when he hit the first grand slam home run ever in a World Series. And in the fourth inning Jim Bagby hit a home run with two men on—the first pitcher ever to strike a home run in a World Series. Now, many other players have achieved both of those feats since, but they were the first and they did it within a few innings of each other in the same game.

I can tell you how that first inning went, don't think I can't. Charlie Jamieson hit a single, Bill Wambsganss singled, Tris Speaker beat out a bunt. First three men up. The fourth man was Elmer Smith. Burleigh Grimes was the pitcher. He got two quick strikes on Elmer. You know, years later, Burleigh and I landed together on the same club, the Yankees. We were sitting in the clubhouse one day and I decided to ask him about something that had been bothering me, bothering me for thirteen or fourteen years.

"Burleigh," I said, "I want to ask you one question. Why in the world did you throw Elmer Smith that high fastball in the 1920 World Series after you had got two strikes on him with spitballs?" He had thrown two beautiful spitters in there for strikes.

"Hell," he said, "I was trying to waste one. It was a bad ball."

"It sure was," I said. And it was. I think it was just about up to Elmer's cap bill. But you couldn't throw a fastball by Elmer Smith. When he saw one of those babies it was feastin' time—he'd go right after it. I've got a mental picture of that ball going over the fence, right now.

I'll tell you another story about that game. We hit Burleigh very hard that day. Which was unusual, believe me, because he was a tough man to hit, with that spitter of his. But we had picked something up. Every time Burleigh was going to throw a spitball, Pete Kilduff, the Brooklyn second baseman, would pick up a handful of sand and throw it down between his feet. Why he did that I don't know. Maybe to make sure his hand was dry in case he had to field the ball. Somebody on our club, I don't know who, noticed Kilduff doing it and so we watched him. I knew it; I watched Kilduff whenever I came to bat against Burleigh. Every time he picked up that dirt and threw it down I knew what was coming. Kilduff could read the catcher's signs, you see. So when he didn't pick up the dirt I knew to expect either the curve or the fastball. We knew when to lay off the spitter and wait for some other pitch to hit. If you wanted to guess, you'd go with the fastball, because that was Burleigh's other good pitch, along with the spitter. So we were in a pretty good position up there against him.

If Kilduff was doing that to make his hand dry I could understand it. Coveleski was a spitball pitcher too. He threw a beauty. He used to spit all over the ball and there were times when you could see the saliva flying off of it when he fired to the plate. There were also times when that ball was hit to me and it still wasn't dry and I'd throw a

Burleigh Grimes. "... that spitball, the famous Burleigh Grimes spitball that was so hard to hit."

spitball to first base. You should have seen the first baseman dancing around trying to catch it! One time the darn thing was so wet that when I picked it up and threw it, it slipped right out of my hand and ended up in right field. When Coveleski was pitching and the ball was hit to me, if there was time I'd give it a little twist to dry it off before I threw it.

The story came out later about how we'd been watching Kilduff, and I'll bet Burleigh's neck turned a little red when he heard about it.

Okay, now we get to the fifth inning. That's one of the top moments ever in baseball. It's got to be, any way you look at it. And I'm standing right there, not more than a few yards away. Boy, it happened so fast—bang-bang-bang—hardly anybody knew what had taken place.

I can remember it just like it happened yesterday. The Dodgers got two men on base, Pete Kilduff on second and Otto Miller on first, with nobody out. The batter was Clarence Mitchell, a pitcher—he'd come in after we knocked out Burleigh. Clarence Mitchell was a good hitter, which is why they let him bat in that situation. Well, he hit it square all right. He drove a line shot that I thought was a base hit sure. No question in my mind but that it was going into the outfield. But our second baseman, Bill Wambsganss, was off and running the moment the ball left the bat. He ran toward second base and jumped just as high as he could and he took that ball right out of the air, backhanded. I can see him yet. In my memory he's still there, stretched out a little sideways in midair, his gloved hand thrown way up, and that ball is stopping dead in the center of his glove.

Everybody in the ball park thought it was going into the outfield, including Pete Kilduff and Otto Miller. They were moving as soon as the ball was hit. Well, Bill Wamby was running toward the bag anyway and he stepped on second and that was two out. But then he started to throw the ball to first base. I had been watching Otto Miller coming down the line—he was running full steam. I yelled to Bill, "Tag him! Tag him!" You see, Bill had run to the bag, made sure he touched it, but hadn't yet looked toward first base. He had his arm cocked to throw, but when he looked around there was Otto Miller, running right toward him. Bill just went up to him and touched him on the chest with the ball, just as easy as saying hello. I think that was the first that Otto Miller realized the ball had been caught. When Bill touched him, Miller stopped in his tracks with the most dumbfounded look on his face. I've always said it was Otto Miller who completed that triple play because he just kept coming, right into Bill's arms. When the triple play had been completed I think Pete Kilduff was still running, around third base. That's how fast it all happened. The whole thing took maybe three seconds.

The jump that Bill made to grab that ball was just unbelievable. What made it possible was he had started running in the direction of second base the moment the ball was hit and his motion gave him just the little extra spring he needed. I'd never seen him jump that high before. Shucks, I don't think I've ever seen *anybody* jump that high for a line drive. Now, if I hadn't yelled out to him he may have thrown to first or he may have not. If he had thrown it would still be the triple play but not unassisted. That was the thing—an unassisted triple play. If it had been a plain triple play with other men handling the ball I daresay there would be some dust on it today; but since Bill did it all by himself it'll be up in lights forever.

For a few moments the fans couldn't quite grasp what had happened. There was a little lull. Then it sank in. You should have seen the scene then! It was the tag-end of the straw hat season and they started throwing those hats all over the field. We had to call time while some men came out with wheelbarrows to pick up the straw hats.

You know, just a little added note. Next time he came to the plate, Clarence Mitchell hit into a double play, first to short and back to first. I handled that one in the middle. So Clarence Mitchell made five outs in two consecutive times at bat.

Anyway, that's the story of your unassisted triple play. Only one ever made in a World Series, and not many others ever made, anytime, anyplace.

We went out the next day and beat them 1–0 with Walter Mails. That put us up four games to two. We still had to win one more. You see, the World Series that year was a best five-out-of-nine deal. They experimented with it that way for a few years, then went back to what it is today, four-of-seven. So the first three games were played in Brooklyn and the next four were scheduled for Cleveland. If there was to be an eighth or a ninth game we would have had to go back to Brooklyn to play.

Walter Mails did a fine job for us that day. I'll tell you something

Bill Wambsganss, left, and his three victims: Pete Kilduff, Clarence Mitchell, and Otto Miller. The mourning band on Wambsganss' left sleeve is in memory of Ray Chapman.

about that game. After he had finished warming up, Walter Mails came back and sat down on the bench. He picked up a towel and was drying himself off. Then he looked around and said to us, "You boys get me one run today and we'll win." I can still remember him saying that. Well, that's just what we got him, one run, and he made it stick. George Burns got a single and Tris Speaker scored him with a double. That was in the sixth inning, and Walter was as good as his word.

The next day Coveleski shut them out 3–0 to give us the championship. As soon as the celebrations were over—it was Cleveland's first pennant and first world championship—I got on the train and headed back to Alabama. My head was still spinning from all that had happened to me. In June, I had been at the University of Alabama, then I went to New Orleans to play, then in August to Cleveland, and in October I'm the shortstop on a championship team. My whole life had changed. I knew then I would never be a doctor. I was a major leaguer now.

I didn't get into a World Series again until 1932, when I was with the Yankees. It was against the Chicago Cubs and it was a rough-going Series, I can tell you. There was a lot of bad feeling on both sides and it just kept on getting worse. You see what happened, late in the season the Cubs lost their regular shortstop, Billy Jurges, to an injury. So they bought Mark Koenig to fill in. Mark did more than fill in; he played great ball for them. He hit over three hundred and fifty and pulled their infield together. A lot of people said the Cubs wouldn't have won the pennant that year without Mark Koenig. But when it came to dividing up the World Series money, the Cubs voted Koenig just a half-share.

Now, Koenig used to play for the Yankees and he still had a lot of friends on the club. So when it came out in the newspapers what the Cubs had done, you should have heard the talk in the Yankee clubhouse. The Cubs were called every kind of cheap, no good so-and-so's you could imagine. "If it hadn't been for Koenig they would be dividing up second-place money." That was the feeling in our clubhouse.

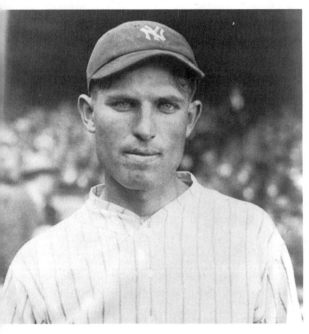

Mark Koenig in 1927

The Series opened in New York. After we'd taken batting practice on the first day, Ruth went and sat in the dugout near the runway where the visiting clubs came out. In those days the visiting club had to come through the Yankee dugout to get to the field. Well, Babe sat there and greeted every one of those Cub players. You never heard such goings-on, such yelling and cussing and ripping. Babe started it and then some of the other fellows picked up on it and they really laid it on the Cubs, because of what had happened with Koenig. Not one of the Cubs answered back; they just went out on the field. But they had to be steaming.

We beat them two straight in New York, pounding them around pretty good. Naturally that didn't improve their disposition any. They had started yelling back and we knew that when we moved on to Chicago it was going to be a rough time, because the newspapers were in on it now. A feud had started between the Yankees and the Cubs and it wasn't going to get any better.

Ruth was doing the loudest yelling. And he could pour it on, too. That was another department he led the league in. And of course the fact that Ruth was involved just made it bigger. Anytime that fellow was involved in anything, good, bad, or indifferent, everybody paid attention. You could love him, hate him, or be neutral, but you couldn't ignore him. There never was such a personality on a ball field. Talking about him can never do him justice. You had to be there, you had to see for yourself.

By the middle of the third game, in Chicago, it had got just plain brutal. I'd never known there were so many cuss words in the language or so many ways of stringing them together. But I'll tell you where it was all heading—right for the history books.

In the top of the fifth inning the score was tied, 4–4. I was batting in front of Ruth and I led off that inning. I grounded out. I went back to the dugout and sat down. Babe stepped up and just the sight of him was enough to set that place to jumping—the Cub players, the fans, everybody. Charlie Root was the pitcher. The Babe took one strike. Then two strikes. With each pitch the yelling was getting louder and louder. Babe? He was just as calm as could be. He was enjoying it all, that son of a gun. You couldn't rattle Babe Ruth on a baseball diamond. No sir!

After the second strike Babe backed out and picked up some dirt. He rubbed his hands, looking square into the Cub dugout. What was coming out of there was just turning the air blue. He looked at Burleigh Grimes who was cussin' at him, and Babe cussed him right back. Burleigh had a towel around his neck, which he took and started to wave. Then Babe raised two fingers and pointed to the center-field fence. After doing that, he got back into the box and set himself. Charlie Root delivered the next pitch. The ball was just above Ruth's

Babe Ruth, right, with Mel Ott. "My heavens, that was some Babe Ruth."

knees. A good pitch, a strike. Babe uncoiled one of those beautiful swings. *Crack!* I can still see that ball going out of Wrigley Field. Have you ever seen a golf ball take off? That's the way that ball shot into the air, just like a golf ball. It got so small in such a hurry it looked like it was shrinking as it went. It traveled out of the ball park and through a high tree standing out beyond. That tree was full of little boys and maybe some men, too, watching the game. When the ball went through the tree every one of them just rained out of there, dropping down to run after it.

By the time Ruth rounded third base it was something to see. The fans were throwing whatever was handy at him—cabbages, oranges, apples, just everything. What a show! What a circus! Babe Ruth. My heavens, that was some Babe Ruth.

After the game, which we won, 7–5, we naturally were congratulating Ruth on having done a good job. He hit two home runs in that game and so did Gehrig, but as usual Ruth was the center of things. Here's what he said:

"I was out at the hospital this morning and I told a little kid I was gonna hit him a home run today."

Mrs. Sewell told me later that when Babe came up in the fifth inning she heard Mrs. Ruth call out to him, "Remember the little boy." And that's when he pointed out and hit the home run. He'd already hit one, but I guess he figured that wasn't enough.

Do I believe he really called it? Yes sir. I was there. I saw it. I don't care what anybody says. He did it. He probably couldn't have done it again in a thousand years, but he did it that time.

That night Judge Landis wrote Joe McCarthy a very severe note, telling Joe to get his players to refrain from all the profanity. He told Joe that if we didn't calm down our vocabulary we would all be fined. You see, the yelling was so loud it was carrying to the stands. My wife could hear it. Joe McCarthy read that note to us in a meeting before we went out on the field the next day. Well, you could have heard a pin drop in our dugout during the game. We sat there like mummies. One thing you didn't do in those days was monkey around with Judge Landis. He was the *law* in baseball.

We let our bats do the talking for us in that game. It was a 5–5 tie into the seventh inning and we unloaded for four. I remember I got a single to right field to score two. I did all right that day, got three hits. We scored four more in the top of the ninth and beat them 13–6. That made it four straight and finished the World Series.

We mauled the Cubs in that Series. We really did. That was a pretty fair hitting team we had. Everybody talks about Ruth and Gehrig, but then just for good luck we had Bill Dickey, Tony Lazzeri, Ben Chapman, Earle Combs, Frank Crosetti, myself. By reputation the 1927 Yankees are supposed to be the greatest ball club ever, but I contend we had a good club in 1932. I may be a little prejudiced, but that was one heck of a team. You look at the lineup we put on the field for the first game of that World Series and you'll see we had six fellows in there who are in the Hall of Fame today—Ruth, Gehrig, Combs, Dickey, Red Ruffing, and myself.

I ought to point out that the Cubs were no patsies. Listen, they were a strong club. They had Billy Herman, Gabby Hartnett, Kiki Cuyler—they're all in the Hall of Fame—Charlie Grimm, Riggs Stephenson. Outstanding players, all of them.

Riggs Stephenson was a good friend of mine. Still is to this day. I can tell you a funny story about him. You know how it is in Yankee Stadium, how when it gets late in the season that sun can bother the dickens out of the left fielder. Well, your shortstop and third baseman can have a terrible time with the sun too, on balls hit up into the air. There are times when you see it and then lose it and just have to take a chance and grab where you think it's coming down. Well, Riggs Stephenson came to bat one time and he hit down on a ball that bounced off the plate and bounded way up in the air toward me at third base. I looked up and the sun was right there. All I had was a glimpse of the ball before I was blinded. I shut my eyes and put up my glove and wouldn't you know but that ball landed right in it. I was the most surprised person in Yankee Stadium. I took the ball and pegged it over and threw Steve out at first. I told him later, "Steve, I can catch those little old hoppers you hit down there with my eyes shut." Which is just what I did.

But he could hit a ball. There weren't many fellows who could swing the bat the way he could. I don't know why he isn't in the Hall of Fame. You just look at his averages sometime. And I'll say this, too, while we're on the subject—my brother Luke ought to be in there. He was a great catcher, year in and year out, and he could hit. A tremendous asset to a ball club. I'm not saying it because he's my brother, but because it's true.

That's right, I didn't strike out very often. I guess more than anything else, that's my reputation today—the man who didn't strike out. Once over the full season I struck out just three times, and then there were three years where I struck out only four times over the full season. Over the last eight years I played, I averaged around six strikeouts a season.

I suppose you've got to be blessed with good eyesight and judgment and coordination. But going way back, I can't remember when I couldn't throw a bottle cap or a rock up into the air and hit it with a broomstick handle. I used to carry a pocketful of rocks around with me and every now and then take that broomstick handle and swat at them. I wasn't training myself to be a hitter; at that time I was no more thinking of being a ball player than I was of sitting on the moon. I just loved to hit at those things and see them go, and it made sense to me that if I wanted to hit them I had to keep my eye on them. That's the secret—and it sure isn't much of a secret, is it? You can't hit that bottle cap and you can't hit that rock—and you can't hit that baseball —unless you're looking at it.

Once I started playing ball around town I realized I could hit. I hit the ball just about every time I swung at it. I could see a ball leave my bat. A lot of people don't believe that's possible. But it sure is. All you have to do is watch it. It doesn't disappear when you put the bat on it. I watched a big league game not long ago and I saw some boys striking at balls that I swear they missed by a foot. They couldn't have been looking at those balls. You just know they couldn't.

The first thing you've got to learn if you want to be a good hitter is where the strike zone is. Another thing you've got to know is what kind of umpire you've got behind the plate. Some are keener than others. If you take a pitch a quarter of an inch outside of the strike zone it's a ball. And a good umpire will call it a ball. You've got to find out who they are and go accordingly. Bill McGowan, Tommy Connolly, they were good umpires. Billy Evans was a good umpire, but he missed some every once in a while. So I knew that when Billy Evans was umpiring behind the plate I couldn't take a pitch real close; not when I had two strikes on me anyway.

One of those years, when I struck out four times, I was in St. Louis and with two strikes on me the ball passed around the bill of my cap. Bill McGowan—who was one of the good umpires—said, "Strike three, you're out, oh my God I missed that." All in the same sentence. He sure had missed it. But I didn't say anything. I just turned and walked away. The next day before the game he came up to me and apologized.

"I did my best, Joe," he said.

"Good enough, Bill," I told him.

There was a fellow named Pat Caraway, a left-hander with the White Sox. He struck me out twice in one ball game. This was in Cleveland. It was a full house out there that day and the center-field bleachers were filled with white shirts. Pat Caraway didn't have very good stuff. You could have reached out and caught the ball he was throwing with your naked hand and tossed it back to him. But he had a herky-jerk motion and that day he was throwing that white ball in out of those white shirts and I never could find it.

Lefty Grove? I'll bet I was up around .400 against him. Sure he was tough to hit. But I could pick up the ball the moment he turned it loose and I followed it right on it. And it came right on in. With Grove you didn't have much time. Whoosh! But I let him furnish the power. All I did was flick my bat out at it and it would go. But he was fast. There were a lot of good fastball pitchers, but they weren't as consistently fast. Grove always was. Inning after inning, he never slowed up. I don't know where he got it all from. He could stand out there for a week and barrel it in at you. Never tapered off. Sometimes when the sun was out really bright he would throw that baseball in there and it looked like a flash of white sewing thread coming up at you.

One of the biggest thrills I ever had in my baseball career was the

Carl Mays

day I went five for five against Grove in Yankee Stadium. The last one was a home run into the right-field stands. When I hit that one Grove threw his glove way up in the air in disgust. Oh, he was sore. When I came around to the plate Ruth was standing there, waiting to hit next.

"Kid," he said shaking my hand, "thanks for doing my job for me."

Babe Ruth and Lefty Grove. Two of the greatest names in baseball. I'm proud to have been on the same field with fellows like that. And Cobb, too, and Speaker and Walter Johnson and Lou Gehrig and Jimmie Foxx and Al Simmons and Harry Heilmann and all the rest of them. Great players and wonderful people. Looking back on the years I see how fortunate I was. And sometimes I can't help thinking how strange the design was. We think we run our own lives according to our own plans. But we don't. Not always anyway. I've often wondered what my life would have been like if a ball hadn't gotten away from Carl Mays in Yankee Stadium in August 1920 and hit Ray Chapman in the head. Because the moment that ball left Carl Mays' hand, my life began to change.

FREDERICK CHARLES LINDSTROM
NEW YORK N.L., PITTSBURGH N.L.,
CHICAGO N.L., BROOKLYN N.L.,
1924 - 1936
COMPILED LIFETIME .311 BATTING MARK,
INCLUDING SEVEN SEASONS OF .300 OR
BETTER. ONE OF ONLY THREE PLAYERS TO
AMASS 230 OR MORE HITS A YEAR TWICE.
AS YOUNGEST PLAYER (AGE 18) IN WORLD
SERIES HISTORY, HE TIED RECORD WITH
FOUR HITS IN GAME IN 1924. EQUALLED
MAJOR LEAGUE RECORD BY COLLECTING
NINE HITS IN 1928 DOUBLEHEADER.

Fred Lindstrom Hall of Fame plaque

Fred Lindstrom

IT'S POSSIBLE that if it hadn't been for that ball bouncing over my head in the 1924 World Series a lot of people would have forgotten I ever existed. The association is made so often: Lindstrom, the bad bounce, the World Series. I still hear about it. Some people think I hit the ball, some think I scored the winning run. I have to refresh them on it. "I didn't do anything but just stand there," I tell them. "It was very easy. Anybody could have done it."

I don't think there's any doubt that baseball is the greatest sport for memories and reminiscing. One story always leads to another. I remember one time my wife and I had driven up to the Canadian Rockies for a vacation. This was years after I'd retired. We were coming home on the west side of the Rockies, into Montana. We were cruising along on the highway and I was listening to a ball game on the car radio. Dizzy Dean was doing the broadcasting. There was a lull in the game because the pitcher had been hit by a line drive and was being administered to on the mound. Having some time that he had to fill, Dizzy launched into a story.

"You know," he said, "this reminds me of the opening day of the 1935 season, in Wrigley Field. I had gotten the first two men out and Freddie Lindstrom came to bat." Well, my ears perked up at that. Here I am, driving along a highway in Montana and my name is coming over the radio.

"Boy," Dizzy said, "what an experience I had that day. I pitched Lindstrom what I thought was a good fastball outside and he wound up and hit that thing like a bullet right off of my knee. It knocked me down and I thought my kneecap was broken. They had to carry me off the field. That goldarn Lindstrom. I'll never forget it."

Well, there's the key right there—baseball people seem never to

Fred Lindstrom

forget anything, whether it be something truly memorable like getting hit by a line drive, or some obscure thing that might have happened fifty years ago and for some reason has become locked in memory. One story or episode associates with another and you can go on forever. It's almost as much fun to talk about baseball as it is to watch or play. That's just one of the many things I love about the game.

My love for baseball was probably unavoidable. I was born and raised on the South Side of Chicago, just a short distance from the White Sox ball field, Comiskey Park. I suppose that automatically made me and everybody else in the neighborhood a White Sox fan. The Cubs were like people in a foreign country, as far as we were concerned.

Being a White Sox fan in those days was very enjoyable. I'm talking about the years during and just after the First World War, when the White Sox had some championship teams, with players like Joe Jackson, Buck Weaver, Claude Williams, Eddie Collins, Happy Felsch, Ray Schalk, Eddie Cicotte. Those were truly great ball clubs and naturally the neighborhood youngsters felt that the world began with them and ended with them. Of course when the scandal broke in 1920 and the White Sox were accused of having thrown the World Series to Cincinnati the year before, I was terribly disappointed. That anyone could, first of all, point an accusing finger at those fellows and then, second of all, substantiate the charges, was quite a disillusioning experience. There is that marvelous story of the young boy who accosts Joe Jackson outside of the courthouse and tugs on Joe's sleeve and says, "Say it ain't so, Joe." Well, that story might be apocryphal, but it nevertheless symbolizes what we felt, because we were so close to those fellows. By close I mean of course from the fan's perspective, and even though that is not at all intimacy it can lead to greater disillusionment because those players were part of our fantasies.

I went out to the ball park to watch them every opportunity I had. I didn't always pay to get in though, because in those days we kids used to shinny over the fence and get into the bleacher seats. The only time we would ever pay to get in was after we had been in the alleys junking for rags and bottles and things of that sort, which we would sell. Once we had raised the requisite amount of cash—two boys under the age of twelve could get in for a quarter—we would head for the ball park and enter like gentlemen. But most of the time we were scaling the wall. You put a big league game on one side of a wall and a couple of baseball-crazy kids on the other and you have set up quite a challenge to those kids' resourcefulness.

Once I got inside I used to stand behind the screen in left field and watch Joe Jackson in the outfield. I always marveled at the way he could take the ball and throw it to the plate. He had an overhand throw and later I found out that this was the correct way to throw the ball from the outfield, getting the overspin on it that would carry it three hundred and fifty feet. And his hitting, of course, never ceased to astound me. Simply one of the greatest natural hitters that ever lived.

I wanted to be a ball player, right from the beginning. When I was attending Loyola Academy in Chicago, Jake Weimer, our coach, who was a former big league pitcher, groomed me as a shortstop and as a ball player. It was Jake Weimer who first imbued me with the spirit of big league baseball.

In 1922, when I was sixteen years old, I had a chance to work out with the Cubs. This was arranged through a friend of Bill Killefer, who at that time was managing the Cubs. I worked out with them in the morning and took batting practice against Virgil Cheeves, who was one of their starting pitchers. I hit a couple of balls real well and felt I was doing all right. When I got into the clubhouse after the work-out, Killefer asked me to write my name down on a piece of paper. When I did that he said, "We'll call you when we need you." I thought that would be next week. I didn't know this was their polite way of getting rid of you.

About three weeks later Dick Kinsella, a scout for the Giants, came through town. He was really on his way to the west coast to do some scouting, but at the behest of Jake Weimer he had agreed to stay over for a day and see me play. I played a game for Loyola that day and in the game I hit four consecutive doubles. I signed a contract with the New York Giants that night, in the Auditorium Hotel. My Dad had to come along with me and sign also because I was only sixteen years old. No, I wasn't disappointed in not signing with a Chicago team. After having been politely shoved off by the Cubs, I felt I was lucky to sign with anybody.

I must admit that my family was not overjoyed by my signing. They didn't want it at all. They wanted me to continue my schooling; but without the desire to learn I don't think I would have been a very good student. I had made up my mind: it was baseball or nothing. My head and my heart were too filled with baseball to make any other decision possible.

At the time I signed with them, the Giants were world champs and were going to be world champs again that year. In fact, they won four pennants in a row from 1921 through 1924. They were the great team of baseball, the glamour team, much as the Yankees became later on.

I played a few games at Toledo in 1922, stayed there the full season in 1923, and in 1924 came up to the big leagues. I was only eighteen years old when I joined the Giants.

John McGraw's Giants. That's what they were called and that's what they surely were. I don't know if any other manager before or since has ever had such a close identification with a ball club. The team reflected in its style of play his tactics and strategy, his ideas and attitudes, his businesslike approach to the game.

It was not an easy ball club for a rookie to break in with; no club was in those days, but I think the Giants were particularly difficult. The young fellows, like Bill Terry and myself, were more or less in another sphere—on the ball club but not part of it. The older players stood apart as a gang of their own and you remained isolated from them. They were a unit—George Kelly, Frankie Frisch, Ross Youngs, Irish Meusel, Frank Snyder, Art Nehf. The closeness was built upon success, you see—those four straight pennants. It took a while before anyone was allowed into that inner circle.

Frisch was a fiery ball player. He gave everything he had out there, but all the same, he and McGraw just couldn't get along. There was constant squabbling between them and they became terrible enemies

Bill Terry in 1924

at the end, before McGraw finally traded him. The problem lay, I think, in a similarity of personalities. They were both fighting types, aggressive and outspoken. McGraw had simply formed a dislike for Frisch and you could *feel* it whenever they came together. They had a brutal argument in St. Louis in '26. The name-calling became vicious. I can remember McGraw finally roaring at him, "You're through!" Ostensibly they were arguing about something that had occurred in the game, but what it really was was that personality clash again. Frisch was traded to St. Louis after the season, for Rogers Hornsby.

Now Ross Youngs, on the other hand, was one of McGraw's favorites. The old man always said that Youngs represented everything that he, McGraw, represented—meaning the bulldog attitude, the fierce determination to win. And Youngs certainly did possess those attributes. If you had nine guys like Ross Youngs on the ball club that club wouldn't need anyone to prod them on to greater efforts. He never stopped hustling, never stopped trying to win. Youngs didn't hustle any more than Frisch did, but he was by nature a very quiet person where Frisch was outspoken, and it was this difference in them that made McGraw like the one while disliking the other.

Youngs was still a young man when he developed a kidney disease in 1926. It began to slow him down, more and more. With a nonstop hustler like Youngs, it became more apparent than it would have with an ordinary ball player. McGraw became so concerned that he assigned a male nurse to travel with Youngs when we went on the road. But Youngs' condition kept worsening. I can remember one day in Philadelphia, at the hotel there, the elevator door opened and he came walking out, accompanied by the nurse. We hadn't seen Ross for a week or so and I was startled by what I saw. His legs were so bloated up that they eliminated the creases in his trousers. That's what the

Ross Youngs. "...one of McGraw's favorites."

Frankie Frisch. "...he and McGraw just couldn't get along."

Hack Wilson. "... losing him was the biggest mistake the Giants ever made."

illness was doing to him. It was a short time later, maybe even the next day, that he was taken to the hospital. This was the beginning of the end. We never saw him again. He sat out the entire 1927 season and then died that fall. He was thirty years old. McGraw was badly shaken when Youngs died. They say only two photographs ever hung in McGraw's office—one of Christy Mathewson and one of Ross Youngs.

We had Irish Meusel in left field. His brother Bob seems to have gotten more publicity through the years; maybe because Bob played on the 1927 Yankees and people are always writing about that team. But Irish was quite a good ball player in his own right. I would say he was as reliable a man as I ever saw for driving in the winning run. Put that winning run on second base with two outs and, boy, was he tough. How would I account for that? I think it's probably psychological. Certain fellows simply respond to the pressure better than others. There was something about those clutch situations that brought out the confidence in Irish Meusel and made him a tougher hitter. Maybe his concentration became more intense, or maybe he was one of those fellows who didn't worry about being up in crucial situations.

And of course we shouldn't overlook a very practical aspect of it: Irish was a good low-ball hitter and often in those situations, with the winning run parked out there, the pitcher will throw breaking balls and try to keep them down. And that was right in Irish's alley.

We also had Hack Wilson on the Giants in those early years, in center field. A lot of people forget that Hack started his career with the Giants and by rights that's where he should have stayed. He of course later became a great star with the Cubs and losing him was the biggest mistake the Giants ever made. You see what happened, McGraw decided Hack needed some more seasoning in the minors and sent him out. But somebody in the front office, through a clerical oversight, failed to protect our recall rights to him and left him unprotected in the draft, and the Cubs picked him up for a few thousand dollars. I can just imagine what McGraw said when he heard about it; he knew what an outstanding talent Hack was.

Losing Hack Wilson was one of the most costly things that ever happened to the New York Giants. If we had had him with us through the late twenties and early thirties we would have won pennant after pennant, because he was having tremendous years—for the Cubs. In '27 and '28 we lost the pennant by two games each time. And we were close again in 1930. With Hack in center field there's no question in my mind but that we would have won in each of those years. You see, we didn't have a good, steady center fielder at that time. McGraw was rotating different men in and out of there. As a matter of fact, he finally pulled me from third base and put me out there. This was in 1931.

Look at it this way. In 1930 Hack set those National League records that are still up there: fifty-six home runs and one hundred ninety runs batted in. Well, if he had been with the Giants in 1930 and done only *half* of that, I think we would have won it. His home run mark may well be broken some day, but the RBI record is just awesome. It's seldom that anybody comes within even fifty of that record.

We had a good, tough team with a good, tough manager. McGraw was tremendously successful with that era of ball player. Later on, however, when he began to be associated with the more modern-day players he didn't have the ability to cope with them. I'm thinking of men like Bill Terry. The players that were coming in had a different approach to baseball—times were changing—and McGraw was just not able to adapt. You see, his style of dealing with someone who had made a mistake on the field was to chew them out unmercifully. He could be brutal. He thought nothing of humiliating a man in front of the whole team. For years he was able to get away with it. But Frisch wouldn't take it, and then Terry wouldn't take it, and I wouldn't take it.

McGraw and I had some very rambunctious arguments. He could be very unfair at times. I would talk back to him at these times, trying to be very logical in presenting my side of the story. But he didn't like that. Of course it wasn't until I felt very secure as a ball player that I started talking back to him. This was in 1928. I had a very good year in 1928, hitting .358, getting two hundred thirty-one hits, driving in over one hundred runs, and had a good year in the field. I resented being second-guessed, which he did on a couple of occasions. I remember one time, with the bases loaded and one out, I picked up a ground ball hit to my left and went to second base to try and start a double play. Well, we got only the top man, missing the runner at first by an eyelash. A run scored and eventually we lost the game in extra innings. Later, McGraw contended I should have come home with the ball. I felt that was second guessing. I didn't appreciate it and let him know about it. We had a loud shouting match over it.

It ate his craw to have anyone talk back to him, to challenge not only his authority but his expertise. But I wasn't trying to do either; I was simply trying to defend myself. Nevertheless he held me in high esteem. I know that, because in 1931 when asked by the *New York Journal* to pick the twenty greatest ball players he ever saw he ranked me ninth on his list.

Finally a hassle began to develop between McGraw and the Giant organization. By the Giant organization I mean Mr. Stoneham, who owned the ball club. This was Charles Stoneham, Horace's father. He decided the time had come to get rid of McGraw, which was not going to be an easy task because the man had been there for so many years and had become an institution. And then it also became a question of who was going to succeed him. It finally boiled down to Terry or me. Well, Stoneham promised me the job. So did Jim Tierney, who was his right-hand man and the club secretary.

As a matter of fact, when Tierney first approached me on the subject of managing the Giants, Terry was in the room. This was in the Alamac Hotel in New York. Terry and I were sitting around talking when Tierney came in and broke the news to us that Stoneham was going to replace McGraw. Both Terry and I said, more or less in unison, "How can that be? McGraw has a contract that goes for three more years."

"True," Tierney said. "But McGraw owes Stoneham $250,000." That was from McGraw's horse racing affairs in Havana. "The old man is going to forget it if McGraw agrees to step aside."

Naturally we were curious as to who Mr. Stoneham had in mind as a successor.

"He does have somebody in mind," Tierney said to me. "You."

"Did he give me any consideration?" Terry asked.

"Yes he did," Tierney said. "But he figured you two fellows were such close friends that you would go along with it."

We didn't have to ask why the move was being made. McGraw had become old and crotchety and had lost much of his effectiveness. He no longer had control of the ball club. But still, he was John McGraw and it wasn't going to be easy to get him to step aside. And if he had not owed that money I'm sure Stoneham couldn't have got him to agree to it.

As I look back upon the situation now and realize how deeply in debt McGraw was, I can see that it was bound to create an unstable position for him to work from. It had to make him less positive in his thinking and less logical in his rationale than he would have been if he had been free of such financial woes. It had to be a major distraction for him as well as a constant source of tension and irritation. You blend that with the normal tensions and irritations of managing a big league ball club and you don't have a very serene situation.

There was no question in our minds that he had lost a lot of effec-

John McGraw. "It ate his craw to have anyone talk back to him..."

tiveness as a manager. As I mentioned before, times were changing, players were changing. It was a different caliber of man now and tactics that had been successful before were no longer applicable. You now had to manipulate your players more diplomatically. I don't mean to imply that you had to coddle them; it's just that the days of brutally dressing down a ball player for a mistake were gone. John McGraw's career had begun in 1891 and been in many ways quite remarkable. It was just unfortunate that he had remained inflexible when everything else was changing around him.

All this was taking place in 1931. That was the season I made the switch from third base to the outfield. Well, midway through the season I broke my leg, in Philadelphia. While I was laid up in St. Francis hospital there, Jim Tierney came to visit.

"We're making that change we spoke about next year," he said. "McGraw is going out and we want to make you manager. We're not doing it this year because of your broken leg. Mr. Stoneham and I have decided to postpone it until next year."

It was supposed to be a secret, but it leaked out and McGraw heard about it. Well, he was quite bitter. He seemed to feel that I had undermined him, which of course was not true. But this was what he believed.

Nothing happened until June of the next year, 1932. Then one day Bill Terry called me into the office at the Polo Grounds, shut the door and said, "They've made me manager."

I was dumbfounded. "You don't mean it," I said.

"It's true," he said.

It was like the grandstand falling on my head. Terry, who was a very good friend of mine and still is to this day, knew that I had been considered for the job and what a terrible disappointment this was to me.

What happened, I suppose, was McGraw continued to believe I had been undermining him and even though he and Terry weren't very good friends had probably been instrumental in selecting Bill to succeed him.

My career with the Giants terminated shortly after McGraw's. When Terry took over the ball club I'm sure he thought it would be better for both of us if I went to another team. So I was traded to Pittsburgh. Two years later the darndest thing happened, or I should say almost happened.

It was November, 1934, and I was attending the baseball meetings. I was having breakfast with Warren Brown, a Chicago sportswriter. Terry came over and sat down.

"How's it going?" Warren asked him.

"Fine," he said. "And I've got a bit of news for you. I'm going to get Freddie back with me on the Giants."

"How are you going to do that?" Warren asked.

Terry mentioned someone on the Giants he was going to trade to Pittsburgh for me.

I didn't say anything. It was Warren who told Terry.

"You're out of luck," Warren said. "A deal has just been consummated. Lindstrom and Larry French to the Cubs for Jim Weaver, Guy Bush and Babe Herman."

Terry looked at me. "Is this true?" he asked.

"A half-hour ago," I said.

Do you know what that was all about? It had been Terry's intention to trade for me to bring me back to New York to manage the ball club, while he would move up to another position with the Giants— I presume general manager.

So that was twice I missed out on becoming manager of the Giants.

It seemed there was always something happening around the Giants during the McGraw years. Sometimes it was due to the force of McGraw's personality, and sometimes there were other factors involved, like what happened at the end of my rookie year in 1924.

After winning a close pennant race against Brooklyn and Pittsburgh —on the last weekend of the season, as a matter of fact—there was some doubt that we would play in the World Series. Do you remember the Jimmy O'Connell scandal? That was really something. It came down to Judge Landis sitting in a hotel in New York trying to decide whether or not the Giants would be eligible to play. For a while there was the clear possibility that he might disqualify us because of what had happened. This was just four years after the Black Sox scandal had broken, remember, and people were very touchy about the slightest taint of suspicion upon baseball.

We had a young outfielder named Jimmy O'Connell. McGraw had bought him from the Pacific Coast League a year or so earlier for a lot of money. O'Connell was a pretty good ball player and a likable fellow, but at the same time he was sort of naive and gullible. Anyway, we were in Philadelphia to play our last series of the season, against the Phillies. If we could beat them one or two games it would assure us of the pennant. The Phillies were a weak club and we were very confident we could run over them without any trouble.

Well, according to the story, O'Connell is alleged to have approached one of the Phillies' infielders, Heinie Sand, on the field before the game. They had known each other in the Coast League.

Jimmy O'Connell   George Kelly in 1921

"Look," O'Connell is supposed to have said, "we're old buddies from the coast. How about looking the other way when the ball is hit at you?"

Sand later reported the conversation to his manager, Art Fletcher, who in turn relayed it to the league president, who in turn informed Judge Landis. Landis came immediately to New York, took a room at the Waldorf Astoria and called O'Connell to his suite. He told O'Connell what he had heard and then asked, "Did you say this to Heinie Sand?"

O'Connell admitted that he had. And then he implicated one of our coaches, Cozy Dolan, and three of our players—Frankie Frisch, Ross Youngs and George Kelly. O'Connell claimed that Dolan had passed the word to him, with the connivance of those three players, to attempt to bribe Sand. He insisted that in the clubhouse they were the ones who had put the idea into his head.

When he heard that, the Judge didn't waste any time. I think it was about two or three o'clock in the morning that he called those three players to his suite. They denied any knowledge of the whole business, were very clear and emphatic about it, and Landis took their word. But when Landis asked Dolan if he knew anything about the alleged bribe, all Cozy would say was, "I don't remember. I don't remember."

That really shook Landis. "You don't remember?" he demanded. "It happened only a couple of days ago and you don't remember?"

Dolan's vagueness didn't sit too well with Landis and he declared both O'Connell and Dolan ineligible. In other words, they were banned forever from organized ball.

You know, the whole story has never ceased to mystify me. Why would O'Connell try to bribe Sand? That was the thing I could never understand. The only explanation I can think of is that O'Connell was, as I said, a naive sort of fellow. And a youngster on that ball club was kidded and booted around quite a bit. There was always a lot of foolery and horseplay in the clubhouse. It's quite possible that somebody might have made a facetious remark and O'Connell picked up on it. I think that's what it finally amounted to, O'Connell taking seriously something said in jest and actually going ahead with it, trying to pull a fast one.

But once Landis had spoken to Frisch, Youngs and Kelly the cloud was lifted and we went ahead. Nevertheless there was a day or two in there when we couldn't be sure what would happen. It was well within his power for the Judge to disqualify us and put the second place team —the Dodgers—into the Series. That would have been a heck of a thing.

So that situation was cleared up and we got set to meet the Washington Senators in the World Series.

I guess I'm still the youngest player ever to participate in a World Series. I was a month or so short of my nineteenth birthday. And all of a sudden I found myself penciled in as the starting third baseman. You see what happened, Heinie Groh, who was the regular at third base, hurt his knee toward the end of the season and was sidelined. This meant that I was going to be the third baseman in the Series, a position I really hadn't played all that much during the season. In fact, I had been a utility man, filling in for Groh at third and Frank Frisch at second. Actually, some people felt shortstop was my best spot. But in any event, I was going into the Series playing a position I hadn't had too much experience at.

Was I nervous? No, honestly I wasn't. I was so young I think I was unconscious of the seriousness of the whole thing. Sometimes a person's innocence can work to his advantage. I was simply unawed by the glamour and unaware of the excitement and unaffected by the tensions that were building up. I was much more excited and emotionally wrought up in the '35 Series when I was with the Cubs, because by that time I was much more familiar with all the trappings and all the seriousness.

McGraw didn't go out of his way to calm me down. In the first place, as I said, I wasn't excited. And in the second place, that sort of thing wasn't done in those days. They just put you on the field and let you play. If you did the job you stayed, if you didn't you left. I can't ever remember McGraw teaching me very much. I think his feeling was that if you wore a big league uniform you were expected to be able to play big league ball.

You know, not only was I playing in a World Series at such a tender age, and at a relatively unfamiliar position, but when I walked up to the plate as the first batter in the Series, who was standing out there on the mound getting ready to pitch to me but Walter Johnson. It was certainly a very special experience, but at the same time I have always contended that because I was so young I was just dumb enough not to be aware of his greatness. To me he was just another pitcher. The fact that he was one of the greatest pitchers who ever lived and that he was supposed to have a fastball that created smoke as it was thrown to the plate did not faze me. As I say, at eighteen I was too young and too dumb to be as impressed as I should have been. But at the same time I had a youngster's self-confidence. I simply thought I could hit anybody.

Johnson was up in years by that time but he could still throw. He had what I would describe as a slingshot delivery. It was a nice, easy movement, which didn't seem to be putting any strain at all on his arm. But he could propel that ball like a bullet. I remember talking once about Walter with Eddie Ainsmith, who had caught him in Walter's younger days. "If you tried to hit against him on a dark day," Eddie said, "you were out of luck. I had all I could do to *see* the ball when he let fly." He said there was many an occasion when he just got his glove up in time, because he actually had not been able to follow the flight of the ball, it was coming in there with such a rush.

You know, it was ironic. Johnson had come to the big leagues in 1907—when I was around a year and a half old—and this was his first World Series. And there I was, just a green kid, playing in a World Series in my rookie year. So naturally there was a lot of sentimental rooting for Walter. All of that was very nice, but neither I nor my teammates shared any of those feelings. We beat Walter in the first game, 4–3 in twelve innings.

I didn't have any luck with Walter that day. He turned me back five times. But George Kelly and Bill Terry hit home runs, and as a matter of fact we peppered Johnson fairly well, even though he chalked up a lot of strikeouts. We pitched a good lefty, Art Nehf, and he went all the way for us.

We had them beat 2–1 going into the bottom of the ninth when they scored a run to tie. Then we scored two in the top of the twelfth and they came back with one and darn near tied it up again. It was a heck of an exciting game and you might say that it set the tone for the whole Series, because nearly every game was nip-and-tuck.

The second game was won by the same score, 4–3, but this time we were on the short end. Again there were some ninth-inning heroics. We were losing 3–1 when we scored two in the top of the ninth. I can remember Hack Wilson rapping out the base hit that scored George Kelly with the tying run. But then in the bottom of the ninth they got a man to second base with one out and Roger Peckinpaugh drove a two-base hit past me down the left field line to win it.

We moved the Series up to New York the next day and beat them 6–4. I drove in what proved to be the winning run with a double in the sixth inning. I really had not done too much hitting up to that point, going something like 2 for 12 in the first three games. But then I got hot.

They beat us in the fourth game to tie the Series at two apiece, in

George Kelly scoring the tying run in the top of the ninth inning of the second game of the 1924 World Series. The catcher is Muddy Ruel. The umpire is Bill Klem.

spite of my three hits. Johnson came back at us in the fifth game and that's one I'll always remember. Against Walter I singled in the first inning, singled in the third inning, singled in the seventh, and then once again in the eighth. It was a nice afternoon's work under any circumstances, but particularly so in a World Series. Four hits in a game is still the record for a Series, one which is held by a number of men. What made it so memorable for me, of course, was getting them against Walter Johnson. And what made it important, naturally, was that we won, 6–2. So that was twice we had beaten Walter, who was such a sentimental favorite.

Then we went back to Washington needing only one more win to wrap it up. The sixth game was a very smooth pitchers' battle. Art Nehf for us against Tom Zachary, two good left-handers. That was a game we should have won. You've heard that one before, I guess. Well, it's true. But I suppose the loser of every 2–1 game ever played has made that statement. Okay, let's give Zachary some credit too. He was a tantalizing pitcher. He had a little nickel curve and a little nickel knuckleball and he seemed to be able to put those pitches right where you couldn't do very much with them.

We scored a run in the first inning on hits by Frisch and Kelly. But then in the bottom of the fifth, with men on second and third, Bucky Harris hit a single to drive them in and there was the ball game. Harris was the manager and second baseman for Washington and he played just a great Series, an inspired Series you might say. He hit a couple of home runs, got a lot of hits, drove in a lot of runs, was outstanding in the field.

Now it was all tied up at three apiece and it was anybody's Series. You know, I have heard people say that that seventh game in 1924 is perhaps the greatest ball game ever played, in terms of importance and excitement and drama. That might be so. It sure had everything. I've always felt that the seventh game of the World Series, which by definition is the most important contest of the season, should be a good one. Well, that game certainly filled every expectation.

Right off the bat there was a tactical battle of wits. A jockeying for advantage. You see, McGraw had been playing Terry against right-handers and sitting him down against lefties. Well, that strategy had paid off because Bill was just beating their brains out. So Bucky Harris did some juggling. He started a right-hander, Curly Ogden, in order to get Terry in there. Ogden pitched to two batters and then they immediately took him out and brought in George Mogridge, a left-hander, one of their top pitchers. That forced Terry out of the lineup in the middle of the game for a right-handed pinch hitter, and when that happened they brought in a right-hander, Fred Marberry, who was another top pitcher.

Did McGraw read it? I can't say for sure what he thought when he saw Ogden warming up. I do know that Washington claimed a lot of credit later on for outfoxing him. And outfoxed he was, because they succeeded in squeezing Terry out of there in the middle of the game. What did I think of it all? Listen, I was that dumb young kid, remember. All I was concerned with was playing my position to the best of my ability and trying to get a few hits to win the ball game. I was content to leave the heavy thinking to McGraw. That's what he was paid his forty thousand for, to do the thinking. And he did it, all of it. Do you know what the cardinal sin was on that ball club?—to begin

Bucky Harris, right, with George Sisler in 1928

a sentence to McGraw with the words "I thought . . ." "*You* thought?" he would yell. "With *what?*"

Virgil Barnes started that game for us. In the bottom of the fourth, Bucky Harris hit a home run to put us a run down. But then in the sixth inning we broke through for three runs and maybe started to smell a world championship.

Then we went into the bottom of the eighth, ahead 3–1. Boy, I'll never forget that inning. You know, what people remember most about the 1924 Series is the ball that took a bad bounce over my head in the bottom of the twelfth and cost us the Series. But not many people remember another bad bounce that occurred, one which was just as important. It was the beginning of a series of events that finally made some of our boys throw up their hands and say, "It wasn't meant to be."

Washington loaded the bases with two out. Bucky Harris came to bat. He hit a ground ball down to me. It looked like an easy chance and I was set to play it when all of a sudden the ball hit a pebble and bounced high over my head into left field. Two runs came in and the game was tied.

So we went into the top of the ninth and here came Walter again, walking in from the bull pen. The Senators had pinch-hit for their pitcher in the eighth, and with everything up for grabs now, Harris brought in his best, even though Johnson had had only one day of rest. It was very dramatic, because here was this great veteran, this fine gentleman, being given another chance to win a Series game.

It was an October afternoon and the shadows were getting longer, which certainly didn't hurt Walter any, the way he could throw that ball.

We had a crack at him in the ninth. Frisch tripled with one out. They put Youngs on first. Then Walter bore down and struck out Kelly and also retired the next batter. That strikeout of Kelly, that was the big one.

It went along to the bottom of the twelfth. That's another one I'll never forget. Not only will I never forget it, but there are times when I still can't believe it. We got the first man out. Then Muddy Ruel stepped up. He lifted a high foul ball over toward the grandstand. Hank Gowdy, our catcher, threw his mask aside and went after the ball. It looked like an easy out. But then the wind began carrying the ball back toward the plate and Hank moved with it. It still looked like an easy out. But then one of those fluke things happened. As he moved under the ball, with his glove up waiting to make the catch, Hank stepped right into that mask, lost his balance, slipped and fell, and the ball came down on the grass alongside of him.

By that time, I suppose, even a callow, eighteen-year-old boy like myself, who knew nothing about fate, should have begun to see the light. Washington was supposed to win this game and that's all there was to it. Because sure enough, given that second chance, Muddy Ruel smacked a double into left field.

Johnson was the next batter. I guess it would have been most poetic if he would have won his own game. But that's not what happened. There was very little poetry in this inning, let me tell you. What did happen was Walter hit a ground ball to Travis Jackson at shortstop.

Art Nehf, left, and Walter Johnson, starting pitchers for the first game of the 1924 World Series.

Jackson booted it. He said later that Ruel, coming down the line from second, had obscured the play for a moment and made him lose the cadence of the ball for just that split second. Whatever happened, he booted it. Ruel, thinking that Jackson would make the play, had reversed himself and gone back to second. So instead of three out, there was one out and men on first and second.

I was standing there with my hands on my hips wondering what could possibly happen next. I soon found out.

Earl McNeely was the batter. Jack Bentley, who was pitching for us, and pitching well, got McNeely to hit a ground ball down to me. Well, it happened again. The ball hit a pebble—maybe the same darned pebble that Harris' ball had hit—and took a big kangaroo hop over my head and went out into left field. And here's Muddy Ruel charging down from second base with the winning run. You know, I don't think he could have scored if Irish Meusel in left field had anticipated my not taking the ball. If Meusel had been running in the moment the ball was hit I don't think Ruel, not a fast runner, a slow runner in fact, would have even tried to score. But Meusel had no way of knowing that thing was going to bounce the way it did. By the time he got to the ball it was too late. He just picked it up and put it in his pocket. The game was over.

So they won it. Jack Bentley, who was something of a philosopher, I think summed it up best after the game. "Walter Johnson," Bentley said, "is such a lovable character that the good Lord didn't want to see him get beat again." You couldn't argue with that. But after all that had happened, I think if Washington hadn't won it in the last of the twelfth, even the Lord might have withdrawn his support of Walter.

No, McGraw didn't have much to say about it. He had seen enough baseball in his life to know when something had been taken out of his hands. You know the old saying, "That's the way the ball bounces." Well, it was never more appropriate than in the seventh game of the 1924 World Series.

As a matter of fact, I didn't talk to McGraw until later that evening, on the train going back to New York. He was in his drawing room with some of his brother Lambs from the Lambs Club who had come down to see the game. He called me in and gave me a couple of shots of bourbon, to get me to quiet my nerves and forget about what had happened. I drank that whiskey on an empty stomach, had no resistance whatsoever to it, and it knocked me out. And I stayed knocked out, all the way home. When we got to New York, big George Kelly picked me up and threw me over his shoulder and carried me through Pennsylvania Station. I guess a lot of people who saw us must have wondered what happened. But it was just a kid coming home from his first World Series.

Index

[*Italic page numbers indicate photos.*]

Aaron, Hank, 69, 137
Adams, Sparky, 189, 193
Agee, Tommie, 105, 107, 110–11
Ainsmith, Eddie, 271–72
Alexander, Grover Cleveland ("Alexander the Great," "Pete"), 14, 27, 28, *29*, 30, 83, 84, *85*, 92, 93, 95, 96, 97, 98, *99*–101, 102, 185, 187
All-Star game (1936), 195, *221*
Alston, Walter, 52, 205, 211, 212
Amoros, Sandy, 52, 54, 55, 213–*14*
Anson, Cap, 116
Antonelli, Johnny, 72, 73
Aparicio, Luis, 135
Appling, Luke, 156–57
Auker, Eldon, 42, 220
Averages, lifetime. *See* Bell, Lester; Kluszewski, Ted; Wood, Joseph
Averill, Earl, *221*

Bagby, Jim, 1st pitcher's home run in World Series, 240
Bailey, Ed, 135
Baker, "Home Run," 8
Bancroft, Dave, 28
Bando, Sal, 59, 67
Barber, Red, 205–06
Barnes, Virgil, *9*, 275
Barnhart, Clyde, 128
Barry, Jack, 18, 27, 28
Bauer, Hank, 65, 80, 81, 213
Becker, Beals, 175
Bedient, Hugh, 171, 176, 177
Belanger, Mark, 110
Bell, Gus, 135
Bell, Lester Rowland, 14, 82–102
Bench, Johnny, 60
Bender, Chief, *170*, 232
Bentley, Jack, 277, 278
Berra, Yogi, 39, 48, 51, 52, *53*, 74, 75, 78, 143, 154, 159, 162, 213
Billingham, Jack, 64
Bishop, Max ("Camera Eye"), 193, 200

Black Sox scandal, 169, 268. *See also* White Sox scandal
Blades, Ray, 187, 193
Blair, Paul, 110, 111
Blue, Vida, *60*, 61
Borowy, Hank, 227
Boswell, Ken, 107
Bottomley ("Sunny"), Jim, 83, 87, *88*, 89, 94, 98, 193, 197
Boudreau, Lou, 144, 145
Brazle, Al, 136
Brecheen, Harry, 136
Bridges, Tommy, 42, 220
Brock, Lou, 14
Brown, Bobby, 153–54
Brown, Mace, 223–24
Brown, Three Finger, 23, 166
Brown, Warren, 267
Buford, Don, 109, 110
Burns, George, 26
Bush, Guy, 268
Bush (Bullet), Joe, 35, 170, *171*, 232
Byrne, Tommy, 14, 37–55

Cady ("Hick"), Forrest, *19*, 172
Caldwell, Ray, 239
Campanella ("Campy"), Roy, 52, 54, 153, 159, 162, 206, 209, *211*, 214
Campaneris, Bert, 167
Caraway, Pat, 252
Cardwell, Don, 108
Carrigan, Bill, 27, 172
Carroll, Clay, 65
Cavaretta, Phil, 14, *216*–29
Chalmers, George, 30
Chapman, Ben, 250
Chapman, Ray, 245, 253; fatal baseball injury, 234–35
Chapman, Sam, 156
Cheeves, Virgil, 258
Cicotte, Eddie, 169, 257; suspension, 239
Clemente, Roberto, 137
Clendenon, Donn, *8*, 107, 110, 111, 112

279